D1204470

CHASING NORMAL

CHASING NORMAL

MY PEER GROUP DESIGN
FOR LIVING WITH BIPOLAR

MICHAEL J. HOFFMAN

MEETING
MINDS

Published in the United States by MHPG, Inc.

Paperback ISBN–13: 978-0-578-61886-9
Hardback ISBN–13: 978-0-578-69104-6

Printed in the United States of America

1st Edition.

Chasing Normal is not intended as a substitute for psychotherapy or professional consultations. Whenever appropriate, please seek medical help. *Chasing Normal* should be used only as a general guide and not as the ultimate source of information on mental health.

The author and publisher shall have neither liability nor responsibility to any person or entity with respect to any loss or damage caused, or alleged to have been caused, directly or indirectly, by the information in this book.

To my mother,
the strongest person I will ever know

Our Mission

To build a much-needed mental health peer support group system as widespread and effective as Alcoholics Anonymous (AA) and other 12-step programs.

Will you join us and help make this happen?

Contents

Before I Begin

This is my story. It could be your story too, or that of someone you know, someone you'd like to help, or even someone you want to make sure you *don't* become.

Now it becomes *our* story which I'm sharing here, whether you've been diagnosed with bipolar disorder or any other type of mental health condition. I am opening up as I never have before with a purpose bigger than myself. This is when I fully jump in.

What Is Bipolar Disorder?

Bipolar disorder is a chronic episodic illness, characterized by recurrent episodes of manic or depressive symptoms. Patients with bipolar disorder frequently present first to primary care, but the diversity of potential symptoms and a low index of suspicion among physicians can lead to misdiagnosis in many patients.

Source: US National Library of Medicine, National Institutes of Health

People with bipolar experience high and low moods – known as mania and depression – which differ from typical ups-and-downs most people experience. The average age-of-onset is about 25, but it can occur in the teens, or more uncommonly, in childhood. The condition affects men and women equally, with about 2.6 percent of the U.S. population diagnosed with bipolar disorder and nearly 83 percent of cases classified as severe. If left untreated, bipolar disorder usually worsens. However, with a solid treatment plan including psychotherapy, medications, a healthy lifestyle, a regular schedule, and early identification of symptoms, many people live well with the condition.

Source: National Alliance on Mental Illness (NAMI)

one

"GET ME OUT OF HERE!"

Checking myself into a local hospital in Beverly Hills seemed like a good idea earlier in the evening but I have a sneaking suspicion that this is going bad fast and I want to go home, except I won't, and now I can't, because I signed a paper and paper rules, and I did this voluntarily, because I know I have to, but do I have to? What have I done?

I thought maybe I wasn't bipolar but now I'm not so sure.

In fact, Cedars Sinai, a well-known, plush facility in Beverly Hills where I thought I'd get the *best* care in the *best* place in the *best* neighborhood, turned me away (insurance!) and sent me 22 miles across the county to a hospital in Alhambra, a suburb in the middle of strip malls, highways, and nothing else that feels even remotely hospitable. Then again, what could possibly feel welcoming when you're wheeled in on a gurney, drugged up and hopeless?

As if I didn't already have enough meds in me, they give me more once I am strapped down and defenseless.

Please, Nurse Ratched, or whatever your name is – you, the one with my life in your hands – please tell me I'm at least getting my own shitty room and that I won't have to share my space with anyone who's actually crazy because that's not me, not by my estimation, and not officially, at least we know that, right?

I had a messed-up week, okay? But I'm not crazy! Maybe I am bipolar and just can't accept it. Couldn't my therapist be wrong?

As soon as I "sign here" I become an *involuntary* patient, even though I've signed there voluntarily. I guess that's because I regrettably mentioned the 'S' word to the RN, whose stone-cold gaze is not exactly welcoming. I bet she earns $40K a year, which doesn't pay enough to be warm or fuzzy and definitely doesn't allow her to be casual in any shape or form when someone uses the word SUICIDE in a sentence, which I just did because that's how I feel, or at least I did a minute ago, and now I'm not so sure anymore; but then again, I'm not sure about anything.

She methodically ravages my belongings, taking inventory of every item, removing my shoelaces, feeding me meds – *MEDS* – how does she know what I need – and she also provides me with a plastic dish of dried-out, tasteless spaghetti and meatballs with thawed vegetables.

This makes me consider suicide all over again. Plus, it's freezing, 'cause it must be 65 degrees and I can only function between 70 to 74 degrees, which is what I *strongly* insisted on two months ago when I was back in New York City at the Equinox on 63rd Street and Lexington Avenue where the manager threw me out partly for being too aggressive about the temperature.

Did I forget to say I'm delicate and fragile? Have I told you I might have been diagnosed with bipolar disorder and that I'm having a particularly bad day, but maybe not bad enough to be checked in here to what I perceive to be – mistakenly maybe, I know – a loony bin of some kind; and I don't need *more* meds, do I?

Maybe the meds are for sensitive people like me who are scared and want to go home, except I can't, for more than legal reasons by now – not by myself, that's for sure.

They say giving me meds is "for my own protection" but I chalk it up to them covering their ass with more compulsory bullshit.

How Did I Get Here?

I shouldn't be here. This is not my scene. Really, it's not, and this is not some elitist thing with me thinking I am better than anybody else. At least I don't think I should say so out loud.

Doubts. I have doubts that I'm in the right place because there was no sign at the front door saying DENIERS WELCOME or NO JUDGMENT HERE.

I just turned 31 and I have a real job. Please call my family attorney. You do it, please, because you won't let me make my own calls until after the morning support groups. I don't care what time it is. My parents need to be made aware of my situation. No one should be in this situation alone. Everyone needs a food referee to call a foul when an RN serves up this chow.

I am so hungry when they finally offer me what they call food. After the initial check-in, it takes one-and-a-half hours for them to rummage through each and every one of my things. I had a full suitcase with me when I arrived because I had been out of town for business and the hospital is short on staff after nine p.m., which is when I arrived on Wednesday, June 19, 2013 – helpless, strapped down like a sick criminal.

They take my electronics too, which means I can't reach the outside world until I am allowed to use a pay phone, which will be tomorrow because those are the *rules*! They have so many rules here, I'm finding out. Even worse, I have several movies to go with my portable DVD player; finding out that I can't watch them now is quite traumatic, at least for now, and now is all I've got.

This feels traumatic and terribly isolating and part of me knows that someday when I look back it will seem so inconsequential compared to what else I am witnessing right now, but who cares about that when I'm bent out of shape at this moment? Somewhere in my mind I should know that I have to go through this whole shit, that it might give me some much-needed perspective. But for now, I can't access that part of my mind at all and it just sucks.

Instead of lying back with a film I'd like to watch I have to sit down in a chair for 90 minutes and watch these people walk by me and right *at* me, as if I am a rare exhibit in a museum they would never visit.

I use the 'S' word again, not because I want to kill myself but because this sponge cake tastes like shit. I bite

4

into it because I have nothing else to do. I spit it out because eating desserts at night makes me anxious. So does being overly rigid. I say the 'S' word because I want to get moved to the suicide ward if there is one, because they must have better food and personal space.

I think I may be in the wrong place with the wrong nurse and the wrong people. I think I'm thinking that because I think there's some special magical treatment I should get because I'm me and not you or anybody else. But the truth is, I'm thinking too much.

I'm special because my parents tell me I am, and I went to an Ivy League school, and I have a high-paying job as a Big Four consultant.

Symptoms

Symptoms and their severity can vary. A person with bipolar disorder may have distinct manic or depressed states but may also have extended periods – sometimes years – without symptoms. A person can also experience both extremes simultaneously or in rapid sequence. Severe bipolar episodes of mania or depression may include psychotic symptoms such as hallucinations or delusions. Usually, these psychotic symptoms mirror a person's extreme mood. People with bipolar disorder who have psychotic symptoms can be wrongly diagnosed as having schizophrenia.

Source: National Alliance on Mental Illness (NAMI)

Below the Cylinder

I can't see the doctor on staff because he won't be available until tomorrow afternoon. Someone tells me I have to remain here for a minimum of 72 hours because that's state law once you're admitted into a loony bin (fine, "psych ward") with no access to the outside world even on an 85-degree sunny day – and that's a best-case scenario.

I'm trying to cooperate because I want phone privileges and to be moved to the unipolar ward where I'm told they have better accommodations, better food, and all kinds of better everything. But I'm doing this on the downlow as I don't really speak much or pay close attention to what's going on around me until I can't help it; because it's all right up in my face.

A middle-aged Hispanic man with a scruffy beard appears out of nowhere, wearing typical mental-patient scrubs as if there is special gear these people wear in this ward, treated with anti-psycho fabric or something like that just in case it's contagious. He's rambling to no one in particular that I can tell, which suggests I should mention this to the stoic night-shift nurse. She must know what she's doing because she is the professional authority figure here.

While struggling to get her attention, I'm grandiosely fixated on the idea that I could run this place and make it a lot more user-friendly, but who am I kidding? I have no present or future, and I still don't have a pot to piss in – literally!

Who am I to judge what should or shouldn't be?

Then I notice the same guy meticulously scrounging through the trash for evidence of my discarded cake. I indulge in this brief moment of levity – even George Costanza would agree that the cake is well below the cylinder, meaning it's certifiably out of bounds for human consumption. But in two swift bites, the remains of my dessert dissolves in his mouth.

Where am I, and what the fuck just happened?

A frumpy, pale woman, 40 or 45, looking as if she's completely ignored even the remotest possibility of sunlight, suddenly enters and demands her meds. She has black teeth, probably from years of smoking and dipping and chewing, and the most impressive blond mullet I've ever seen. How did she escape from *Duck Dynasty*?

A dangerously overweight, young black woman in stretched-out Spandex pants they wouldn't even sell in a dollar store, encircles me, staring into my sedated eyes as if I'm a forbidden candy apple.

I can feel myself slipping away and hope she doesn't enter my stupor. I've heard people don't leave too easily once they enter your floating stupor. They just hover there, inside your shit, reminding you that you are not alone whether you like it or not.

I don't know whether this is good or bad, but it's definitely not for me to decide.

What other disreputable creatures lurk behind these closed doors?

This could be *One Flew Over the Cuckoo's Nest*, except I lack Randall McMurphy's charisma; or it could be *Good Will Hunting*, except I'm not a math genius like Matt Damon; and I'll never be lucky enough to have Robin Williams as my therapist, the one who unconditionally *gets* me.

7

I know that something wrong in me makes me need to be here. I asked for this, I know, even though I have no idea what I am asking for or what it means or who I will be when I finally get to leave.

Rejecting the Unipolar Ward

The meds calm me down and I fall asleep on a dank cot in a 65-degree room, surrounded by three strangers who smell like they each took a dump in the corner and let it fester. As I contemplate that, guards come by every 15 minutes and shine a flashlight into my eyes, just to make sure I'm still alive. It would be so inconvenient if I die on their watch. All the paperwork. Ugh.

Even with the noise, lights and constant interruptions, I sleep through the first courtyard visit of the next day, which I gather started off with a bang and a whimper at six a.m. When I finally stand up, I see the same Hispanic man scurrying down the hall balancing five cups of decaf coffee to substitute for real caffeine before waking everyone else up who is not totally comatose.

As soon as I got here, even as I was choking on what failed to be a lovely piece of sponge cake, my goal was to get moved to the unipolar ward in the other building. It is the reward for going infraction-free for 24 hours straight and attending all four therapy sessions.

Mission accomplished!

While waiting for my turn to be moved, we, the obliging ones from group, crowd together to watch game seven of the NBA finals, enjoying life like I wish I had done at a bar two nights earlier when this latest spiral began.

Game seven! That is drama, but not like this, being in a hospital because my life has bottomed out.

Mania

To be diagnosed with bipolar disorder, a person must have experienced at least one episode of mania or hypomania. Hypomania is a milder form of mania that doesn't include psychotic episodes. People with hypomania can often function well in social situations or at work. Some people with bipolar disorder will have episodes of mania or hypomania throughout their lives; others may experience them only rarely.

Although someone with bipolar may find an elevated mood of mania appealing – especially if it occurs after depression – the "high" does not stop at a comfortable or controllable level. Moods can rapidly become irritable, behavior unpredictable, and judgment more impaired. During periods of mania, people frequently behave impulsively, make reckless decisions, and take unusual risks.

Most of the time, people in manic states are unaware of the negative consequences of their actions. With bipolar disorder, suicide presents an ever-present danger because some people become suicidal even in manic states. Learning from prior episodes what kinds of behavior signal "red flags" of manic behavior can manage these symptoms.

Source: National Alliance on Mental Illness (NAMI)

Basketball presents an image of great camaraderie. Now it's bristling with the finality of game seven when everything is on the line for those teams but not for us watching, but yet we are so invested, as if it will matter for us. The next season starts from scratch in less than four months, so you have to have a short memory. These guys – these freaks of nature – must struggle to get back to the same place, but why do I care about them when I have more immediate problems of my own?

That's just it. Watching the NBA provides a refuge from the bouncing ball inside my brain – another freak of nature with far less to offer – ricocheting me from one moment to another.

When I venture to the unipolar ward during half-time, in place of a full group of manic outcasts I see an old man occupying the only space in front of the 20" TV, watching *National Geographic*. WTF!

I'm gonna flip out because the game's not on! Maybe they should have a show about us, the lost creatures of a great society, hidden away where we won't be missed. But not now, 'cause I need my hoops!

I feel so out of place and quickly realize what I've given up. I'm freaking out, losing control all over again. It's not a medication problem this time. It's my Basketball Jones kicking into full gear.

I beg my way back to the more chaotic ward, with bipolars, borderlines, schizophrenics, and drug addicts. It takes them 35 minutes to secure a new room for me – meaning precious moments of basketball lost into the ether – but they make it happen because they can see how desperate I am to get back there.

Turns out I've missed the entire third quarter, but I finally get to share in the fourth with like-minded fanatics. And even though my team loses, at least I got to watch it and feel a sense of purpose again.

Reality sets in while LeBron James hoists the MVP trophy. Fuck! My boys are going fishing and I'm stuck in a psych ward.

Next season?

I'm still trying to process what tomorrow looks like. I'm projecting and rejecting and subjecting and objecting and I haven't even washed my face. All I can think of is who I neglected to call, what to tell them, and how they will react.

For starters, I need to tell them that I'm in a psych ward because I have bipolar disorder.

Diagnosis

To diagnose bipolar disorder, a doctor may perform a physical exam, conduct an interview, and order tests. While bipolar disorder cannot be seen on a blood test or body scan, they can help rule out other illnesses that resemble the disorder such as hyperthyroidism. If no other illness or meds are causing the symptoms, a doctor may recommend mental health care.

To be diagnosed with bipolar disorder, a person must have experienced at least one episode of mania or hypomania. Mental health care professionals use the Diagnostic and Statistical Manual of Mental Disorders to diagnose the "type" of bipolar a person may be experiencing. To determine what type of bipolar a person has, mental health care professionals assess the pattern of symptoms and how impaired the person is during their most severe episodes.

Source: National Alliance on Mental Illness (NAMI)

Sharing My Shit

It's time to share my experience with most of these people I just met. I am pretty aware of what to expect from earlier sessions where I was half-paying attention. I broke the ice with some of them the night before, so I am not *too* opposed to it. But bonding over sport is one thing – I'm not thrilled about having to share my shit with people I don't think I'll relate to. Many of them can't sit still for five minutes let alone an hour.

How is this supposed to work? When did someone decide that it would be therapeutic to have total strangers share their life story with other people they have never met? And who would be willing to do that besides strangers who had no other choice but to share their guts and glory because it was either their only opportunity to be heard by anyone, or their last chance to save themselves?

In spite of my own resistance, which is not in short supply, which partly explains why I'm in here, I am finding camaraderie with what I initially perceived to be people living at the bottom of the barrel – their barrel, not mine.

This shows for sure that I have so much to learn, because we're all in the same fucking barrel. I may look to those barrel-dwellers like a less-than-cool dude myself, so I have to swallow that and reboot my elitist bullshit brain.

For a moment I wonder what I would do if I was running this group. Would I welcome people I felt nothing in common with, as if we belonged together? I'd like to think I would, but I honestly don't know if I could avoid judging people; but they are probably used to that. Though it's also possible they were once enjoying a place of prominence before their chemistry sent them flying downward until they ended up in a place like this – a lower-functioning treatment center in a decidedly low-rent facility.

For me, a relatively high-functioning person who comes from a middle-class household, this was a lot to take in.

So why do they put all of us in one group? Maybe that's all they can afford to do for space and money reasons, but here we are, people struggling on social security disability checks, about to slip through the system if one little thing goes wrong. We are people like me, struggling with bipolar, depression, anxiety and other disorders, and working a job so we don't depend on the state, and we are people who end up in hospitals over and over again because we just can't stop contemplating suicide and causing self-harm.

I suppose the world needs to reach out to the ones who fall through society's cracks, first by accepting their insurance or lack of it, and then by actually listening to them as equal human beings.

Now it's my turn to do that by opening my heart and mind to people who may be no different from me at all, especially once you see beyond the surface shit, which means little to nothing when all is said and done. When it comes to addressing our mental health, I believe that whether we like it or not, we're all in the same boat.

My Psycho Solstice

At this stage allow me to introduce the other desperados of sunny Southern California. We are all here during the three longest days of the year, June 20, 21, 22 – my psycho solstice.

Are these my people?

Hayley's warm smile says, "I could hug you right now for not leaving me for good." Hayley is the first person I connected with here. Her look refers to the 45 minutes I trialed the Unipolar ward where I immediately felt out of place in that much too subdued environment. I returned as fast as possible to the hype and havoc of my newfound group.

No matter what, you can find comfort in a group.

Hayley is a drug addict who OD'd. She's an irrecoverable alcoholic looking to escape reality, 22 years old with FUCK and ME written between her two fingers. I don't have any idea what exactly motivated her to do that, but she's making a statement. I see another tattoo on her forearm, which appears to come from prison. It reads *Nobody's Nothing* and the words are surrounded by an anchor. Hayley says she has cirrhosis of the liver already and has no more than 20 years to live. She's a pack-a-day smoker. Marlboro Reds. Hayley didn't eat the hospital food for two days because she won't eat anything unless she knows where the food comes from, as if that makes a difference. But for her I guess it does, and since I'm becoming more open to her, I want to know how she feels about everything.

Uh-oh, am I falling for a smoker?

On paper, I am repulsed by Hayley. So why am I so intrigued by her in here? What is she triggering inside me that causes so much conflict? I'd been on 40 to 50 dates (serial online dating from hypomania) before I met Anne in Turks and Caicos. Anne is perfect looking, without any discernible flaws. Hayley has acne and her head is partially shaven from a recent hypomanic episode. She has vulgar tattoos. Anne has a degree from the top school in Montreal. She speaks fluent French. Why Hayley? She failed to take a college course. What makes her perfect for me with all of her imperfections? Why do I need her to stay an extra day? What makes her so quick to want to stay when I express my desire? It's not my touch because there's absolutely no human contact allowed here. None.

Why is it so painful when she leaves prematurely to return to the man I surmise is assaulting her, who continues to enable her pathology? Did she tell me half-truths as she was reaching out for help? I have her phone number. She makes sure that I memorize it. Should I call her? This whole situation goes way beyond responsibility and logic.

I know nothing of human behavior.

Group gives me a different perspective on life. Being in one forces me to become empathic, to see life through other people's eyes.

Who would have thought my best bud in the ward would have two Aryan tattoos? Iron cross swastikas, to be exact. I think. I don't have the internet in here to confirm. The schizophrenic sees them from the corner of his eye.

"Heil Hitler! Heil Hitler!"

He screams and makes the inappropriate gesture. I want to pretend I don't see it but the damage is done.

What isn't permissible in here?

Maybe ego?

Human nature takes us to great lengths to fit in. The Aryan Nation, fraternities and sororities, sports leagues, dating the wrong person just to be accepted by somebody, and support groups to be with others who empathize. Why begrudge others for taking the same measures I do but to a greater extent?

Group sure does make you think!

Aryan friends? What next?

Most people I know can't confront the world as it is, let alone deal with some Hitler wannabes. I can't wait to hear what they think if I told them about my experience here in this pseudo freak show.

I am safe in here because there is community and camaraderie.

A broken, middle-aged ex-prostitute with visually noticeable STDs tells me her life story before she leaves. Until then, before breaking into tears all she mutters is how her ex-fiancé left her. I think she opens up because I hadn't judged her, not visibly or verbally at least, and found ways to include her. She tells me all that stuff because I have "kind eyes." Prostitution was her form of therapy. The men used her for their therapy, to escape from their world. She tells me this and hugs me tight. This is the only form of affection she shows anyone and it happens really fast and it's over so no one objects to her breaking the rules.

Peter shuts off like he took an oath of Omertà. He seems to find comfort in me from discussing a fading interest in film – a quick side chat during therapy – and then tells me he is a rapist and has served time in prison. I don't respond. I don't judge. When we depart, we shake hands and wish each other well.

Should I wash my hands after shaking the hand of a rapist?

Julian beat the shit out of his brother for bringing heroin back into their mother's life, which infected their mother with HIV. He uses his time here as an escape from skid row and to make us laugh and maybe feel as if we are becoming a little better off than we were before, which is definitely true.

Justin slit both wrists yet loves life two days later. When he removes his bandages, no one disapproves. I thank him for showing me the 26 stitches in each arm. He explains in this matter-of-fact way that he also downed rat poison in case slitting his wrists didn't get the job done. That's literally a lot to digest. Then he reports that the charcoal they gave him to shit out the poison was agony but necessary; and I have to agree.

I see myself here somewhere.

Justin is so similar to me. He quit his job that he loved – carpentry, building with his hands, all that – because he felt so invalidated three weeks earlier during some incident that never needed to blow up, but it did. And here he is, almost two wrists dead and figuring out what to work on next and if he'll be alive to see it through.

What am I afraid of for myself?

Why should I be afraid? I'm in group, thinking about how I used to hate smoking. Now I embrace it because if that doesn't kill me, something else will. So why be afraid? Smoking now reminds me of the freedom we had on the patio together – me and my group bud, my smoking buddy. This is where warmth, empathy, and camaraderie show their faces in a way I don't see or have on the outside. I've since switched to cigars, but no matter. It's the inhale and exhale and the pause in between when the world feels for that one moment as if it's better aligned – and livable, manageable, survivable.

Back in the circle, 46-year-old Luis tells me in his own staccato way that I remind him of his son, also Michael, and that I am a "beautiful person." This is okay because it's genuine. It's fatherly. I can feel that energy coming from him in a real delicate way. He wants my shirt because it belongs to me. That's a new twist, but in the situation we are in, I submit.

Group pushes my buttons.

I have money. I buy Cokes for everyone in the ward. Even someone I've never spoken to thanks me and pats me on the back. The money means nothing to me. The gesture is everything. A little kindness goes a long way.

I'm feeling some real shit so I guess I'm not a lost cause.

Rachel has a dissociative identity disorder. We bond over sport. When I ask her name, she stares at me blankly from five feet across a ping-pong table outdoors where we stockpile our recreation. They put this thing conveniently here, maybe to stimulate us, I don't know, but Rachel says nothing and doesn't blink. She takes another drag from her cigarette – so much smoke, not enough air – and continues to mutter incessantly. When her shots miss, I toss the ball back to her to try again. When my shot misses, she hits it back to me harder than the last one. That's how we communicate.

Morgan is a 39-year-old stripper who looks every bit as good as Marisa Tomei in *The Wrestler*. While I appreciate her teasing the hell out of us, knowing it is impermissible to touch I also wish she would stop. I hope she knows we appreciate her dry wit since she says her family takes it for granted. I'm not judging her, even though I may look like I'm doing that because of the way I'm looking at her, and I hope she knows that and doesn't mix up my staring at a stripper for appreciating her sense of humor.

Kristen, with her six amputated toes – five on one foot because of her diabetes – sneaks in a bite of chocolate and cookies from other patients while hoping for the best, some divine intervention maybe, to stave off high blood sugar and her depression. I wonder if and how her family copes with this.

There's a lesson here, somewhere....

Depression

The lows of bipolar depression are often so debilitating that people may be unable to get out of bed. Typically, people experiencing a depressive episode have difficulty falling and staying asleep while others sleep more than usual. When people are depressed, even minor decisions such as what to eat can be overwhelming. They may become obsessed with feelings of loss, failure, guilt, or helplessness; this negative thinking can lead to thoughts of suicide.

Source: National Alliance on Mental Illness (NAMI)

Stuck with Myself

I witness one of my roommates sleep 22 hours a day. He was a zombie when I arrived and still a zombie several days later when his parents come to visit him. I can't tell if they are heartbroken or just tired or both.

Having a family is risky.

Maybe I shouldn't be so hard on my brother back home when I lecture him and try to make him alter his habits. That bird on my shoulder is worth listening to – at least until it craps on my shirt.

In this minute, I love being inside. The rest of the world can treat me like my brother sometimes has, not unlike lots of older siblings, I guess.

Manipulate me. Exploit me. Bully me. All with no consequence. Possibly helping to trigger or craft my bipolar. And yet, I forgive him for it!

This family stuff is hard. I don't know what it's like to be a parent, but I see the potential for heartbreak. I've seen it in my own parents when I struggle, and this episode right now won't help.

Every decision has consequences. Can I handle the stress of having a family? I want to be stable enough to do that, but right now I'm afraid to have a family of my own. I believe I can't have a wife, let alone a child, until I'm stable enough to be in a healthy relationship. With myself first.

One step at a time.

I am validated when I make baskets, at one point 18 in a row from the top of the key. I rock. I swish. I bond. I enjoy my talent for playing ball, checkers, and chess with other patients. This success validates everything I know to be true that the rest of the world has overlooked and exploits. They don't really know me or *see* me. If feeling validated makes me more giving and kind, feeling invalidated makes me alone and miserable. And that sucks. The outside world can sometimes make me feel even less than the shit expunged from Justin's rectum.

But enough about Justin's rectum.

I don't need validation all the time. I just can't have it *none* of the time. Maybe I should be more lenient. If my new roommates had what my co-workers have – a healthy baseline for sustaining their mental health and unconditional support – then maybe they would be as superficial, too.

Maybe that's how the world works. People are just playing their part and they're not so willing to recognize others, like me, trying to do the best they can.

Why judge people for being who they are?

We're all chasing normal.

We can all be ourselves in here, where it appears to be safe. And it is so far, at least for me. Some people are pretending they feel safe, until they realize they really can just be themselves here at the Alhambra Medical Center and pretend no more.

On the outside, I was pressured to conform to lofty expectations that chipped away at my self-worth, compromised my values, and destroyed my self-esteem.

Thank you, Alhambra, for bringing me back to myself.

Martina's family feud brought death to her family. A cousin shot her, shattering her insides and leaving her near death while causing interminable knee pain and scoliosis. She says she forgives her cousin and they get along well today. She lives for her children and grandchildren.

Maybe this level of restraint, strength, and selflessness can come only after having a family of my own.

This thought is horrible and hilarious at the same time. The timing is never perfect. You never know when a loved one may shoot you, ignore you, or tell you you're shit.

Treatment

Bipolar disorder can be treated and managed using:

Psychotherapy, such as cognitive behavioral therapy and family-focused therapy.

Medications like mood stabilizers, antipsychotic medications, and antidepressants.

Self-management strategies such as education and recognition of an episode's early symptoms.

Complementary health approaches such as aerobic exercise, meditation, faith, and prayer can support, but not replace, treatment.

Source: National Alliance on Mental Illness (NAMI)

We All Need a Fix

I think twice about skid row and homeless people. How can America, the greatest and wealthiest country in the world, cut off healthcare at age 27 unless we work for the *right* company? Will that company cover our insurance when the rates go higher? How about when mood disorders cannot be treated effectively and culminate in chaos? The forum helps to discuss these topics constructively, but where will we all go from here?

Those who need, cannot afford. Those who have, ignore.

Why should I be so fortunate? I've hated the people I work with who can't go an entire day without discussing their hair, the beach, or conflicts with two weddings on the same weekend, while they ignore or judge everyone who does not fit their image of how we should look or talk or laugh or live our lives.

Maybe I'm right to despise small talk. Maybe the corporate world is not conducive to wholesomeness.

Before I came here, I forgave my brother to appease my mother. Now I have forgiven him for *me*, so I can move on. I have a grip on that finally, and all this other stuff I am learning from Peter, Julian, Justin, Luis, Rachel, Morgan, Kristen, Alhambra, and the desperados who don't say their names. I tuck away these feelings and swear I will hold on to them.

These people matter because we are all desperados.

Before I leave, I attempt to throw away my pants with no drawstring and these funky running shoes with no laces. The RN stops me.

"Someone else can use these."

"Who?"

She doesn't know, but someone will. I pack up and make sure I don't leave anything behind because if I have to come back here it might get too comfortable.

Elijah, black, about my age, severely malnourished with two healed-up slash marks on his neck, runs up and down the hall in my shoes. He looks happy. I think I'm pleased that the nurse's recycling project is working, and so fast, even before I'm out the door stepping into a world I once knew before, but in different shoes. I wonder for a second if I am walking differently now, after these groups and the whole experience.

I experience a euphoria going from a highly uncomfortable and insulated place to freely discussing my issues with total strangers *because* they don't judge me.

Can I sustain it? Can I replicate it?

The hospitalization helped me accept the fact that I am bipolar. It has started me on a more structured and committed regimen of treatment using medication. I see my three days here as absolutely necessary for my development. It has taken me from a raw place of acknowledgment to the necessary step of acceptance.

Acknowledgment. Acceptance. Action.

Most people avoid hospitals at all costs, which may be to their detriment. I'm here to tell you that it can be rewarding, even if the stay is as short as mine. By the time I left I was in such a good place: Full of curiosity and a willingness to engage more constructively with others.

I continue to learn by listening and keeping an open mind. This is a lifelong process to find solutions to different problems, a process that doesn't end until we take our last breath.

But not so fast.

First, I can share this new rehash of old themes with my parents to remind them that I am not a lost cause, not by any means, not at all, in fact. Even though they know that and continue to root for me, a little reminder can't hurt. It's for all of us.

No judgment! This is the key.

In fact, in a few months from June 2013 to October 2013, I will be asked to go through facilitator training at a prominent non-profit mental health peer support organization, designed for people like myself battling bipolar and depression.

I'm finally accepting of my diagnosis. The psych ward stay, even for just 72 hours, helped me get there.

The hospital and the groups completely changed my approach to how I must work on my mental health. It's time for a total reboot.

two

HOW I LEARNED ABOUT MOOD DISORDERS AND THE POWER OF EMPATHY

There are two reasons I can think of why I don't tell people how to manage their mood disorder:

1. I am not a trained therapist or life coach.

2. I don't know how to live other people's lives better than they do. Telling people what to do assumes we do.

From my experience, guiding and advising is more effective than telling. People need to learn for themselves so they can apply what they learn.

So, I won't advise anyone. I will, however, openly share from my lived experience. This is where I have some expertise. From that I hope you learn a great deal.

I've been fighting this mental health battle long before I wound up in the psych ward – way before anyone suspected anything; not my friends, not my teachers, not my family. People thought I was a little *different*; I knew it was way worse than that.

Understanding Root Causes

Sometimes I define my struggles as BD (Before Diagnosis) and AD (After Diagnosis), with a little bit in between, as in that gray area which occurs every now and then out of the blue, and has me wondering if I need to start psychoanalysis all over again.

What can explain this latest relapse?

That's just me, but odds are, by you reading this, it could be you or someone you know and are looking to help.

My diagnosis has forced me to deconstruct my life experiences and find more effective coping strategies through a combination of clinical treatment and non-clinical support.

Here's a quick breakdown:

Clinical treatment includes psychodynamic therapy, psychiatry, cognitive behavioral therapy, and dialectical behavioral therapy.

Non-clinical support includes 12-step programs and peer groups.

Through a mix of these influences, I have spent years on a roller coaster of constant change: taking meds, rejecting meds, taking new meds, doing more therapy, doing less therapy, learning to listen, deconstructing what I was hearing, grudgingly accepting what I was hearing, eventually identifying patterns, assessing my negative thinking, taking responsibility, and after several years, began to benefit from more rational and logical avenues to lead a more fulfilling life.

Like most people with these struggles, different forms of psychodynamic therapy provided the great jumping-off point to explore the foibles of my childhood and how they still affect me, even when I think I'm over it.

As one of the world's most famous (fictional) therapists, Dr. Jennifer Melfi explained to one of the underworld's most famous patients, Tony Soprano, "Understanding root causes will make you less vulnerable to future episodes."

(Fun fact: I should mention I have *nearly* total recall of every movie and TV show I have ever seen. The mind is a strange organ.)

Through therapy, I've learned to reconstruct a series of disjointed, seemingly unrelated events in an effort to realize how my issues, which began to surface at a young age, have impacted my thoughts, emotions, and rash responses.

As I revisit old memories, my reaction has been similar to Tony Soprano's:

"My fuckin' head is spinning."

It would have been easier to detect my mental health issues from one bad incident rather than from a culmination of many, like someone experiencing PTSD from military service, something most people can relate to and accept.

In my case, my disorder formed because my early struggles were not acknowledged, accepted, or resolved.

My early therapy was full of venting and rejecting rather than learning how to cope and strategize. I lacked a community to relate to and felt little to no camaraderie with my circle of friends, which left me feeling invalidated and isolated.

I blamed myself, but the reality is, I didn't know any better.

Causes

Scientists have not yet discovered a single cause of bipolar disorder. Currently, they believe several factors may contribute, including:

Genetics:
The chances of developing bipolar disorder are increased if a child's parents or siblings have the disorder. But the role of genetics is not absolute.

A child from a family with a history of bipolar disorder may never develop the disorder. Studies of identical twins have found that even if one twin develops the disorder, the other may not.

Stress:
A stressful event such as a death in the family, an illness, a difficult relationship, divorce, or financial problems can trigger a manic or depressive episode. Thus, a person's handling of stress may also play a role in the development of the illness.

Brain structure and function:
Brain scans cannot diagnose bipolar disorder, yet researchers have identified subtle differences in the average size or activation of some brain structures in people with bipolar disorder.

Source: National Alliance on Mental Illness (NAMI)

My Timeline

When I first shared my timeline with a friend who didn't know my backstory on how my mood disorder ballooned, she made two good points:

1. Events during my childhood sound like a lot of people who aren't bipolar. Why do I have bipolar?

2. How can a parent or therapist make the distinction between a pre-teen going through normal stages of adolescence from one in the early stages of a mood disorder who needs to have his or her mental health addressed as soon as possible? Isn't it disastrous to assume the worst and put every kid on meds?

Great observations!

After much thought, here is my response:

There's no perfect equation or input-output. When it comes to what you experience as a kid and the impact it has later on, that's true across the board. That's why pre-empting a mood disorder is so tricky.

I believe it is as difficult to predict if someone will have bipolar or depression when they are in elementary school as it was for economic forecasters to predict the market crash in 2008. Many signs were there in hindsight, but how many experts accurately predicted the subprime mortgage crisis?

As for diagnosis, consider your *average* 10- or 12- year-old, and his or her *normal* range of behavior and personality. The normal range of behavior for one child tends to be quite different from the other. The clinicians assessing their mental health will also treat them differently. Their initial assessment – the *label* – will stay with the parents and the kid forever.

That said, I believe my mood disorder is linked to a combination of circumstances, genetic makeup, and confusion – mostly racial – that were addressed poorly at the time and left unresolved.

I would (and probably could) list every incident but I was told more than once that it would be overkill, so I focus on those that stand out.

Here is my abridged version taken over several years from excerpts in diaries, notebooks, Evernote, text docs, rambling emails, text messages, and backs of napkins:

Early Childhood Sibling Issues
Most of us with siblings had problems with them growing up. My *typical* older brother enjoyed being king of the castle after school each day. He didn't manipulate me so much as take advantage of the situation.

According to my parents, my brother was never comfortable sharing the spotlight with his kid brother. When I first came home from the hospital his first words to my parents were, "When is he going back?"

It wasn't until my twenties that I could understand sibling rivalry. When you're seven, all you know is that your brother is picking on you and your parents won't do a goddamn thing to stop it. They had jobs, and when they came home they were simply too tired and busy with other things to pay close attention. They didn't see the sibling torture I was going through.

If I reacted to my brother's bullying, it only reinforced him to continue. But how can you not react – especially as a kid – if someone wants to get under your skin? Someone living under the same roof will always find a way.

My parents often told me to defend myself – not physically, but mentally.

Ignore him!

Why don't you just walk away?

At the time, I wasn't strong enough mentally to do that. I didn't have the power or ability to control the situation on my own. My parents were too busy earning a living to address my incessant tirades and too tired to address my complaints when they came home hungry and needing to relax. Most younger siblings could get over this, but for whatever reason I could not.

Today, my bipolar manifests through anxiety, short temper, and rapid cycling (alternating between highs and lows). Experts attribute this type of chronic behavior to upbringing. I agree! I also wouldn't be surprised if this sounds familiar to lots of people with older siblings.

Like many younger brothers, I became a victim.

Location, Location, Location

I grew up in a white, Jewish suburb of Philadelphia, which messed with my sense of identity. Today, my mom is still one of just a few black people in the neighborhood. It's safe to say there aren't many black Jews anywhere.

Manifesting My Insecurity

My heritage contributed to my mood disorder. I battled the weirdness that is so inherent in this country, especially a generation ago, of being a person of mixed race.

This was before it was seen as fashionable!

I have never felt a genuine part of any one community, which created an unresolved sense of insecurity.

This didn't happen overnight.

I often wonder which interactions directly or indirectly contributed to my current condition more. We were a solid family. My parents worked in sales and real estate. They were and continue to be loving human beings.

At a young age, I was bullied for my looks – a little dark, a little light, but mostly somewhere in between. Since no one knew how to categorize me, they filled in the blanks with their own bias which made many awkward and uncomfortable moments.

One early example comes to mind. In fourth grade, some kid called me black boy, over and over during a recess. I don't know why I hated it, as it was partially true and I loved my black family, but to this day I can still remember who said it, the look on his face when he did, and how I still have violent bouts in my head about what I'd like to do to him.

A year later, my fifth-grade classmates told me I should date Tiffany, who was the only black girl in my class – as if I were ready to date and she was my only choice.

I repressed a lot of these feelings since I didn't have an outlet to express them. I think I'd be too ashamed to, even if I did.

Early Warning Sign for Mood Disorder
I was a pretty good student until middle school. My history and math teachers agreed that I worked hard but got discouraged easily.

I spent six hours writing out word-for-word and trying to memorize the Bill of Rights after missing an assignment. I needed constant validation to offset feeling like a failure.

I cursed out my seventh-grade science teacher when I was too agitated to explain that I deserved extra credit for leading an assignment that my lab partners received. My parents still remember the distressing phone call from the assistant principal.

"Michael called Mrs. Nestor 'a fucking bitch.'"

The extra credit would have given me a B for the year. My mom told me that if I got a C I would have to go to summer school instead of enjoying my first full summer at overnight camp.

Rather than try to address the discrepancy rationally, I shut off for thirty minutes, lashed out at my septuagenarian teacher on the verge of retirement, and endured six weeks of summer school.

Nice job, Hoff!

Then There Was Basketball
I occasionally had meltdowns when my team lost. This wasn't just the usual throwing a hissy fit. Since my father worked during the week, he and I spent all day Saturday watching each team of middle-schoolers play from 9:30 am to 4:30 p.m.

My dad and I became obsessed with the league (I'm not sure which of us was crazier). We perfected a scouting process by marking down where the top players shot the ball, attacked the basket, and how the coaches constructed their defensive schemes (2-1-2, man-to-man, 1-3-1 trap at half court).

Bipolar Never Sleeps

In a crucial game, I got ejected when a boy who flew under our radar stripped the ball from me on consecutive possessions and I tried (and failed) to dropkick him.

Before I could play again my father made me apologize to the player and the referee since I cursed him out too when he threw me out of the game.

At 12 years old you get second chances.

Called an "Oreo"

During freshman year in a public high school, I was too academic minded for any of the black basketball players to accept me as a peer. They called me Oreo (black on the outside, white on the inside). I was also too talented at basketball for any of the honor students. They too called me Oreo – but behind my back! I couldn't win either way.

Dove into Race Roulette

I had never done any public speaking until I delivered a speech at a B'nai B'rith Youth Organization (BBYO) event on the topic of, "Would Jews lose their identity if they marry a gentile (non-Jew)?" I felt like I had to volunteer since I had been battling with this my entire life. In many of their eyes, I wasn't Jewish since my mom had never converted. Whatever. I stuck up for my family.

Even though we all had eight minutes to present, I spoke incongruously but poignantly for barely one minute after everyone else argued a Jew and a gentile should not marry, with some variation of "they'd lose their identity."

I explained that my parents are not only different religions; they are different races. Interracial marriage did not become legal throughout the United States until 1967. I resent that because it is still not acceptable in many circles. I wouldn't be here today if it still stood.

I finally got to bare my soul for a throwaway exercise in front of a bunch of strangers.

I got second place, and though reluctant at first and nervous as hell, they appreciated my point of view. It felt good to be accepted for being different.

Played Basketball at a High Level

As a freshman, I played well with our BBYO team, featuring a bunch of upperclassmen who would go on to play Division I college ball. It set me up for acceptance with the guys and new opportunities with the girls.

Hit It Off with a Girl – Finally

My luck began to change when I paraded around with the *popular* Jews at the next BBYO event. I was Mitch Kramer in *Dazed and Confused*, if you exchange the pool hall for the Jewish Community Center.

Just when my newfound popularity allowed me to bond with a real girl, a chapter leader told a joke with the word "Shvartze" in it (loosely translated as the n-word).

Parents of my buddies were so appalled they cancelled our dues and pulled us out of the chapter. Without their participation, I was gone too, which meant a quick start to a new cold streak.

Even then, I would have loved to give my desert-dwelling brothers a second chance. I wanted so badly to be there.

At the time, I knew staying with them could have helped elevate my social standing, but it left me frustrated on several fronts.

Transferred from Public to Private School

In 1997, during my second semester of freshman year, I *escaped* the basketball culture at Lower Merion High School (LMHS), where Kobe Bryant (apologies for the shameless name-dropping) had just won a state championship the year before. When you have the best high school player in the country, a ballplayer's time is committed to the school from the minute the final bell rings straight on through until 10:30 p.m., leaving *no* time for schoolwork. My parents convinced me to take an entrance exam to a top private school because of the ridiculous schedule at basketball-centric LMHS:

2 p.m.: Miss eighth-period class and take team bus to away game.

3 p.m.: Junior Varsity (JV) team dresses, goes through strategy, and warms up.

4 p.m.: JV game. Varsity must watch JV through half-time before getting dressed.

5:15 p.m.: JV showers and recaps game.

6 p.m.: Varsity warms up for game. JV must stay to watch Varsity game.

7 p.m.: Varsity game.

8:30 p.m.: Varsity showers and recaps game.

9 p.m.: Kobe Bryant stays for interviews, talks to media, college coaches.

9:45 p.m.: Both teams take mandatory bus back to school.

10:30 p.m.: Team gets home from away game.

10:45 p.m.: Eat dinner. Do homework, if still functioning.

The coach and school officials justified this demanding schedule because they were in the national spotlight. Their success drew people from other districts to rent or lease houses in Lower Merion in order to have their athletically gifted children compete at this *dynasty*. The school leaders encouraged it. My parents knew better than to jeopardize my education and encouraged me to break the pattern.

Had to Handle Occasional Regret for Leaving the Team
Sometimes I wish I had stayed, played ball as well as I had been, and reaped the reward of being treated as otherworldly in high school. At the very least, success on the court would have done wonders for my social life and strengthened my relationship with my brother by playing with him.

Struggled to Find the Rim

I never found similar treatment at my private school, Episcopal Academy, where I had to start over. I didn't make the varsity basketball team because I had spent three months running cross-country instead of working on my jump shot. I had four turnovers and airballed a three my first game because I could not find my rhythm.

Asked Everyone to Play Chess with Me

After that messed-up game, I was like a drug addict, needing a fix to validate my shortcomings on the court and balance me out in general. I tried everything I could to connect with people and feel confident and competent. It's ironic how a game I love so much could make me feel so much heartache.

Not Ready for Summer Camp

With no more summer school needed to motivate me, I worked as a summer camp counselor after junior year. It didn't take long to realize I was too immature to co-exist with other counselors (understatement, it took three hours).

I still had no experience with girls and didn't drink, which made it difficult to bond with the college kids and *cool* high school counselors. I also couldn't take care of 12-year-olds when I still relied on my parents, teachers, and coaches to coddle me.

I hit it off with a female counselor at a mixer but found out a few days later that she hooked up with my co-counselor. Her cousin, a male counselor I barely knew, had told her to stay away from me because I was a "loser." She avoided me at the next event.

I got so heated coaching against him that I yelled at one kid to "strip the ball from his fucking hands when you double him," and when that didn't motivate, I cried out, "He fucking sucks!" at the top of my lungs.

Clearly, I was not much of a role model.

After we lost, I popped the kid's birthday balloon – the only thing that held up after the game. I slept outdoors and enjoyed my solitude in nature to accommodate the campers' and co-counselor's non-verbal cues.

The third night, a senior counselor dumped a bucket of cold water on my face to cap his inebriated night out with the boys. I felt like I was drowning. I stayed up all night in a bunk across camp with my flashlight pointed at the door.

I despised the head of camp, and everyone likely in the know, for not probing who did it. I begged my father to drop everything to drive three hours north to pick me up and bring me home. He said he only would if I promised to find a job back home, among many other conditions. I would have agreed to anything to get the hell out of there.

I started a destructive pattern by not addressing my underlying issues with stress and adversity head on. Instead, I began falling further down a spiral of negativity and into a pile of shit.

Manic Mr. President

I attended my junior prom without a date. On a dare, I did

a dance move called "The Running Man" to the pseudo-rap music (a generous distinction) of Vanilla Ice. My classmates loved it! I broke the ice on the dance floor to allow them to break in their sexual adventures.

Embracing my newfound popularity, I composed an offbeat campaign speech to the 95 percent white Christian community when I ran for Senior Class President. Among the many memorable and outlandish statements, I declared that my black Jewish heritage was necessary to lead the 215-year institution into the 21st century.

I won by a landslide. I also received multiple detentions when, in front of 500 students and teachers in Chapel, I spent several minutes defending the new girl I was "in love with" in a cryptic speech. I thought she had been mistreated by her classmates, like the way I had been for being *unique*.

When confronted, I said it was the Christian thing to do. It was also extremely grandiose, embarrassing to me, and worse, to her. Needless to say, my heroics fell flat.

Worked My Behind Off to Get into a Top School
While continuing to strike out with the girls and riding steerage on the varsity basketball bench, I devoted more time to schoolwork.

When I got accepted to three of the top universities, my friends told each other that I got in only because of affirmative action, the policy that favored minorities. They couldn't say it to my face but made sure that word got back to me.

Now, years later, I have few friends from high school. I've held a grudge ever since.

Tried to Make Sense of Adult Bigotry
Around the same time during my last few days of high school, my buddy's mom who was drinking a double Stoli on the rocks at 3:30 p.m., complained loudly about her daughter's dating preferences.

"Why can't she date someone her own race?"

She meant white and Jewish, not the Samoan guy her daughter was hooking up with. When she realized I was in the room, she paused, put down her glass, and swore she didn't mean to offend me. It was completely offensive, but I appreciated her honesty. Most people weren't that direct to my face.

Are people really this liberal and open-minded as long as it doesn't impact them?

Unfortunately, I'm still trying to figure that one out.

Bloomed Late and Started Drinking
Shortly after graduation in 2000, just a few months before college, I totaled the family car because I was too hung over to drive. I didn't react too well. In fact, I blamed the other driver who broke his leg in the head-on collision, even though it was completely my fault.

That week, I flipped over the living room couch when my parents wouldn't drive me to my summer office job. I cursed them out for 10 minutes straight until they relented. My first major episode culminated a week later when I stayed up all night staring in the mirror in disgust; and then I shaved my head.

Forced to See a Psychotherapist

My parents sent me to a therapist six weeks before my first year of college. After the second session he connected my anger, drinking, and anxiety, and concluded that I wasn't ready for college.

His words were that I lacked the emotional maturity.

My parents dismissed his strong recommendation for social, practical, and financial reasons.

They were more concerned with the backlash from taking a gap year. This just wasn't done. Everyone knew where everyone else was going to college – and bragged about it, in my case.

My high school has a strict policy that everyone must go to college to maintain its 100 percent attendance record and to compete as the #1 private day school in the state.

Also, I attended one of the top private schools in Pennsylvania (which now costs $50K a year). There had to be a return on investment.

My dad thought the structure would be good for me.

It would have except I was too immature to find and maintain it.

He knew too many people who had taken a gap year, never went back to school, and then floundered their way through life.

Good point! Except I did not have what it took to rise to the occasion.

My dad also knew several financial whizzes who made multiples more and advised him to send his son to Wharton.

Why waste four years at Duke or Brown getting a liberal arts degree?

It sounded miserable hearing secondhand that I would be "wasting my time outside business" so I succumbed to the wise counsel of the finance gods who didn't know me and had no stake in my future.

Nothing else mattered but attending one of the top universities listed in the latest AP Poll; and Ivy League institutions made everybody happy.

Everybody but me.

Psychotherapy

Psychotherapy, support groups, and psychoeducation about the illness are essential to treating bipolar disorder:

1. Cognitive behavioral therapy (CBT) helps change the negative thinking and behavior associated with depression. The goal of this therapy is to recognize negative thoughts and to teach coping strategies.

2. Family-focused therapy helps people with bipolar learn about the illness and carry out a treatment plan.

3. Psychotherapy focuses on self-care and stress regulation, and helps a person improve his or her self-care, recognize patterns of the onset of the symptoms, and manage stress.

Source: National Alliance on Mental Illness (NAMI)

Incorrectly Diagnosed with Depression at 18
Identifying an underlying issue is typically a good thing, but it sent me on a decade-long journey trying the wrong meds (anti-depressants) and targeted therapies.

College Struggles
I fell into some bad habits treating college more like John Belushi in *Animal House* than Sean Astin in *Rudy*.

Learned helplessness.

Excessive drinking.

No routine.

I didn't realize the impact drinking had on depression. I didn't know how important it is to have regular sleep.

I dumped my therapist because he didn't say "hi" to me on the street (I later found out that most therapists do not acknowledge their patients outside the office to maintain confidentiality).

A group of peers I could speak to on campus without judgment could have helped me when I believed one of the world's best university hospitals was useless.

After a tumultuous but not completely disastrous freshman year of drinking too much and failing to get past the sixth week pledging a fraternity, I went all out to improve my GPA.

I memorized 73 PowerPoint slides for a Marketing 101 exam. After reciting the first 45 slides from memory to half the library, I envisioned my career as a marketing genius.

This is what I was born to do.

I received a C.

The same tactic would have landed me straight As in high school, but it didn't gel at the top business school in the country where I had to actually *apply* what I learned.

At 19, I was convinced I couldn't compete with all the five-year associates, the junior VPs at Goldman Sachs and JP Morgan, second-year law school students, and all these top international students with 10 AP credits and near-perfect SAT scores.

My high school friends were right. I got in only because of Affirmative Action. I didn't belong.

I had stopped competing because trying and under-performing crushed my self-worth. At least if I stopped trying, I wouldn't be a failure.

Learned to Compensate – or Not

I founded and joined several clubs in college. I became VP of the Chess Club, President of the Wharton Society of Option Traders, Penn Poker Club co-founder, and Student Activities Council (SAC) Secretary. And I started Wharton V, an adjunct organization for five business clubs full of options traders, finance wunderkinds, and marketing gurus. I scheduled our meeting times to align with the games of Philadelphia's Big Five Basketball Association. (Let's hear it for Penn, Lasalle, Temple [my parents' alma mater], Villanova, and St. Joe's.)

My GPA suffered because of these worthless endeavors, but they boosted my ego in the short term. The poker club I founded drew in hundreds and tied together back alley (i.e. dorm room) games by the time I left. The options club helped members receive full-time job offers at top-tier investment firms.

All of this took a toll on me and those around me, too. I was such a pest, pushing everyone to abide with my obsessions. I was desperately seeking validation at everyone else's expense.

SAC strategically increased the number of people who could run on the council to ensure I would be voted out. I was so disgruntled with other heads of clubs who didn't prioritize Wharton V events over their personal lives that in front of a large symposium – with the Dean of the Wharton Business School present – I made sure they knew how I felt.

Couldn't Interview Effectively on Consecutive Days

I landed a few good interviews at investment banks and consultancies – the ones who didn't ask to see a transcript. If I had one good interview, it was rare. And whenever that happened, I would be too manic or depressed in the next one to land the job.

College Girlfriend Told Her Parents About My Background

They said that she'd need to choose between me and them – so we broke up. I had enough credits by then and graduated a semester early because I found the whole experience tortuous.

Lived at Home with Parents

I had to because I didn't have a job or a future. I finally landed a job with a third-tier software company that missed payroll on a few occasions. I made $36K a year. My peers were making at least double that in New York City as they fast-tracked their way to senior management.

Moved to New York City
I was 25 when I started a new job at a fast-paced financial software company, supporting hedge funds with real-time trading. I responded to at least 100 calls and emails a day, most of which reminded me how useless I was. You need thick skin in an atmosphere like that. If you ever want to know what it feels like to be torn a new asshole, try failing to address a trading issue of an intense millionaire trader, precluding him from adding even more money to his billion-dollar portfolio.

I didn't have thick skin and often had inappropriate fantasies that wouldn't have been well-received in that environment, let alone by the police and mental health authorities.

One revisioning has me taking one of the eight brand new HD computer monitors from the traders' and portfolio managers' workstations and beating them senseless until they couldn't distinguish profits from losses and were reduced to cleaning my 325-square-foot apartment.

My overzealous imagination got me through those 10-hour days where I felt emotionally abused by clients and relegated by my ultra-charismatic fast-tracking co-workers who saw me as a weak link on the team and a huge pain in the ass.

Struggled with Alcohol Dependency
I coped through homicidal ideating and drinking, which triggered several more hypomanic and depressive episodes.

Fired Multiple Times
I've worked 14 jobs since graduating college. My longest stint has been two years, and my shortest employment lasted 10 weeks.

What has this Done to My Self-worth?
Unless you are completely delusional (clinically or not), the worst part of being fired is the discomfort you feel weeks in advance, knowing you are on the verge of losing your job, knowing that your bosses and co-workers see you as incompetent and expendable, while your co-workers are appreciated and can't do anything wrong. You have to look at their smiling faces each day, knowing you are one frown away from getting the axe. These are people you spend significantly more time with than your own family.

Then the moment comes when you are officially fired and have to pack it all in and leave the premises. You immediately go to the next place to convince them you are not incompetent, that you are not all the things your previous employer has been telling you for the last several pay periods, which you then realize you will miss going forward. You go into the new place with a gung-ho attitude on the outside, while feeling totally dispirited and broken on the inside. You end up distancing yourself so far from your emotions that you become completely detached from the world to prevent an emotional outburst. You end up doing extreme things just to feel something – or you flip-flop by overcompensating to fit in.

This has happened to me five times already, and I

continue to do everything I can to make sure it does not become six!

Threatened by a Doctor

During my early days attempting to get sober, all it took was one crazy, extremist doctor (I'll call him Doc) who I picked out of a telephone book and ended up believing in wholeheartedly after just one session because I was feeling so vulnerable.

At our first meeting, he told me that if I had one drink between that first session and the second scheduled for two weeks later, he would never see me again.

For Doc, my sobriety was all or nothing. As he framed it: If he told me he did heroin only one night a week, implying that it's fine, since he did not do it the other six days of the week, then I would not want to see him again.

The comparison sounded extreme, but he got his point across.

I'm so glad I met Doc. I'm also glad some therapists just tell it like it is.

Became a Cash Cow

Until that time, most therapists treated me like a cash cow. I shoveled out $175 a session twice a week to talk, listen, and spin my wheels, instead of recommending that I not drink for a few weeks to compare how I feel, and then allow me to decide what is more important – my mental health or my false sense of a social life.

I believed Doc when he said his goal was to make sure that I never needed to see him again.

Most people don't try to sell you on not giving them your business!

He was selling me on a better life.

Related Conditions

People with bipolar disorder can also experience:

1. Anxiety

2. Attention-deficit hyperactivity disorder (ADHD)

3. Post-traumatic stress disorder (PTSD)

4. Substance use disorders/dual diagnosis

People with bipolar disorder and psychotic symptoms can be wrongly diagnosed with schizophrenia. Bipolar disorder can also be misdiagnosed as Borderline Personality Disorder (BPD).

These other illnesses and misdiagnoses can make it hard to treat bipolar disorder. For example, the antidepressants used to treat OCD and the stimulants used to treat ADHD may worsen symptoms of bipolar disorder and may even trigger a manic episode. If you have more than one condition (called co-occurring disorders), be sure to get a treatment plan.

Source: National Alliance on Mental Illness (NAMI)

Diagnosed with Bipolar Type II

Shortly after I flushed all the alcohol from my bloodstream – which I was told could take as long as six months – I was diagnosed with Bipolar Type II. Until then, doctors could not make an accurate assessment because there was so much else going on – like alcohol and an inconsistent sleep schedule. I accepted that drinking can lead to depression, and acknowledged that I fit some of the criteria for Bipolar Type II, specifically my mixed episodes (experiencing mania and depression at the same time). But I felt like I had sacrificed enough by not drinking, which all but destroyed my social life. I wasn't willing to do much else, like taking another medication.

After a few more hypomanic episodes – cursing out my parents, shutting people out of my life, and suffering at work – I agreed to see a new therapist and meet with other strugglers like me.

Began My Shift to Stability

In 2012, at 29, I attended my first peer support group at the Mood Disorders Support Group (MDSG). I attended on and off for 18 months but didn't commit until after my hospitalization. I agreed to go through facilitator training, even though I felt like a hypocrite running groups while I was fucking up at work and getting fired.

I became one of the more effective facilitators because of my hypersensitivity: I recognized when and how to encourage vulnerable members to share their experiences, and when to interject mine to keep the discussion going without monopolizing the discussion. My experience with cognitive and behavioral therapy certainly helped too. I even took over a work-related topic group that focused on interpersonal relationships, coping strategies to prevent harmful episodes, and managing emotions after getting triggered.

I was asked to coordinate when the site directors stepped down the same month. I coordinated weekly to ensure groups kicked off and ran well; when there was a changing of the guard, they asked me to join the board.

I also managed the organization's operations, directed both sites, and received the title Head of Operations, reporting to the Chair and Vice-Chair.

Part of me thinks it wasn't difficult to rise in the ranks because I attended group often, was accountable to my higher-ups, and did what was necessary. Most people hanging around were more motivated to remain on Supplemental Security Income (SSI) than making Managing Director at a Fortune 500 company.

The other part of me is proud to say that I was disciplined: I attended group Wednesdays and Fridays for several years, facilitated good groups, ran the sites, stayed active on the board, built the new website, and handed out pamphlets to welcome new members. I encouraged partnership with other organizations. I presented the group's benefits to outpatient programs. I took time to meet with troubled members before and after group.

Learned to Go the Extra Yard

On several occasions, I stayed after group, even until midnight, talking to one of the many troubled members. One woman didn't speak during group. My instincts told me she wanted to but couldn't. When I asked her if I could help in any way she hesitated before opening up.

"Well, there's this one thing," she said, and then we spoke from 9:30 to 11:45, with me still in my chair and her standing by the door talking through issues she had never shared with anyone else.

On another occasion, I ran a one-on-one *Friends and Family* group with one father who asked me how I manage my entire life since his child was my age and he wanted my insight.

Some facilitators don't reveal much about themselves; I'm an open book. We spoke openly from 7:45 to 10:30.

I've accompanied members to the hospital, sometimes staying with them in the waiting room for several hours working through their plan, and visited them if they were admitted. I did all this on top of my full-time job. I know how important it is to have someone to listen to – *without* judgment.

I report this not to pat myself on the back for my dedication and hard work, although a little patting never hurts. The truth is, when I'm in a good place I identify more with the second statement about myself – proud and grateful for the opportunity. When I'm not in a good place, I know it because that's when I identify more with the first statement – that it was handed to me *only* because I was stupid enough to take on a ridiculous amount of responsibility for an unpaid position.

Got Deep into Behavioral Therapy
Someone in my group with borderline personality disorder had significantly improved her emotions and personal relationships through behavioral therapy and explained that it could also be effective for bipolar disorder.

At her suggestion, I purchased a $20 Cognitive Behavioral Therapy (CBT) workbook on Amazon and completed a few exercises. This helped, but I needed other people to practice with.

I enrolled at the American Institute for Cognitive Therapy (AICT). I spent the first six months working through Dialectical Behavioral Therapy (DBT) exercises that covered four modules:

Mindfulness: Become non-judgmental and present in the moment.

Emotion Regulation: Become more wise-minded and less emotionally reactive.

Distress Tolerance: Increase tolerance to triggers.

Interpersonal Dynamics: Form strong relationships, make value-based decisions.

I worked with a small group of people who attended the mandatory weekly group and one-on-one therapy.

Behavioral therapy has done wonders to help me recognize my triggers and to react more effectively in the moment. For one, taking an *opposite action* is a better approach for when I'm triggered than acting on impulse.

The therapy disregarded why I have a mood disorder – chemical imbalance, conditioning at a young age – and focused on how my erratic thoughts lead to emotional outbursts. The practice helps me redirect my thoughts so I can make more rational decisions.

It was easy to pick up because Marsha Linehan, the founder of behavioral therapy, is a huge *Seinfeld* fanatic. She made learning about all these concepts enjoyable.

Became My Best Monitor
I use my therapy sessions, my support groups, and my CBT exercises to keep myself accountable and as a barometer for my moods. Perhaps the barometer shows that I am stable:

Cognitive Behavioral Therapy (CBT)

CBT is an effective combination of talk therapy and behavioral therapy. CBT is a type of psychotherapy in which patients reframe negative thinking patterns into positive thoughts. Transforming one's thoughts will ultimately result in positive actions and behaviors in difficult moments.

CBT can be useful to individuals suffering from eating disorders, depression, and anxiety. During CBT, patients have the opportunity to work with a therapist to find the source of negative thinking and transform those thoughts into a positive growth mindset. The ultimate goal of CBT is to replace negative thoughts and actions with productive behaviors that make the individual feel equipped to overcome any difficult moment.

Individuals will recognize how their thinking influences their emotions and will establish personalized coping mechanisms. Working with a therapist to find effective and personalized coping mechanisms will ultimately help individuals identify and manage thoughts, emotions, and behaviors in real-world situations.

Source: Psychology Today

not too sunny, not too cloudy, feeling mild winds perhaps, but overall quite temperate. However I feel at any moment, I see my path clearly, and I can accept it.

Why are Mood Disorders So Difficult to Diagnose?

Physical ailments are universally understood. Most people recognize when they are on the verge of getting sick, even at a young age because the symptoms are noticeable. Before you catch a cold, you usually get a sore throat, headache, chest congestion, chills, or feel lethargic. When you are sick, everyone can see that you have a runny nose and are coughing and sneezing. A doctor can feel your head and take your temperature to confirm your weakened immune system.

The steps to combat a cold are clear-cut. You take time off work so you don't get sicker or infect anyone else; you get more sleep, double up on blankets, eat soup, go to a steam room, take cold medication, and suck on cough drops. If your fever runs for more than a few days, you might see a doctor for antibiotics or drink brandy like Paulie did in *The Godfather*. That's an action plan everyone knows and can follow.

Mental illness on the other hand, is tricky. It is not nearly as transparent for the individual or the doctor. Early warning signs and symptoms are not universal.

According to Healthline, "Testing for bipolar disorder isn't as simple as taking a multiple-choice test or sending blood to the lab. While bipolar disorder does show distinct symptoms, there's no single test to confirm the condition. Often, a combination of methods is used to make a diagnosis."

So how do we get correctly diagnosed? The leading method is a mental health evaluation by a trained physician. Unfortunately, this is not a straightforward process. Even if you see a good therapist, how you describe your symptoms – days or weeks after an episode – is often significantly different than how you experienced it in the moment when you felt emotional and behaved irrationally.

Own Your Snowflake

There are 168 hours in a seven-day week. We spend 167 of them on our own and roughly one hour a week in a therapist's office, trying to figure out how to label and treat our issues or for some level of checkup and a bit of maintenance while in their care.

These professionals can only treat us based on an hour a week, so the *magic* they can do is quite limited. We get frustrated sometimes when they give us a diagnosis or prescribe a medication that's different from what we had expected. From the patient's standpoint, wouldn't it be better to provide a detailed account of our mood swings outside their office so they can treat us more effectively when we're in it?

My approach: Journal and share *everything* between appointments, focusing on how specific incidents impacted our thoughts, emotions, and actions, which is more constructive than verbal brain dumping.

For example, we could say, "I was so tired waking up on Tuesday to get to work," or "I couldn't get out of bed until 10 a.m. Could it be medication? Depression?" or "I had to drink instant coffee on Wednesday to start my day, it helped, but I don't want to be dependent on caffeine every morning from now on."

However we phrase our experiences – own it. At a Friday afternoon appointment, or any time we meet, it's unlikely we'll recall important details as accurately as we experienced them over the previous 167 hours. A journal is a good way to keep everything organized.

There are many risks we run into if we do not create a detailed account between appointments.

Let's say on the way to the doctor's office someone bumps into us on the subway and it gets us riled up.

When we share how our week has been, we come off sounding more aggressive than we actually had been. That exchange leads to being diagnosed as bipolar, when really we were just frazzled by rushing to make our appointment on time.

Or worse, maybe the doctor suspects we have a deeper-seated issue, something bordering on paranoia, such as thinking we may feel like the stranger on the subway was put there by some divine intervention to remind us that we don't deserve to be happy.

In those moments, when we believe the universe is against us, we need to develop a *healthier perspective.*

Keeping a journal allows us to be completely focused on our agenda – that we set for ourselves – so when we are asked how our week has been we can respond with something like, "Some idiot bumped into me without saying 'excuse me' a few minutes ago, and my heart is beating a little faster because I couldn't get here on time, but besides that I've been pretty good."

Without the detailed account, we could be fed an unfriendly cocktail of meds for bipolar, anxiety, and paranoia because the doctor writes prescriptions based on what they see. We take these for a few months, and because we are told it's better to go up in meds rather than go off them (so the doctor is not culpable?), we become a walking zombie with no highs or lows and then we are deemed a *success* by our therapist and psychiatrist for no longer having episodes – all because we took a crowded subway rushing to an appointment to save $6 on a cab ride. This might seem dramatic, but this was me!

To echo Hayley's tattoo (Chapter 1 group), "F- me!"

I offer this perspective in group (paraphrased of course) when someone implies that they are *therapy resistant*. This is an important issue for many people who tell their stories to a medical authority and get misdiagnosed or over-diagnosed simply because they lack perspective and over-dramatize their thoughts and emotions. This is especially risky when doctors see their client for only an hour a week and cannot see the full picture. I suggest it's a shared problem that both parties need to pay more attention to in order to set the stage for a more accurate and helpful assessment.

Lest we forget, we hire them to treat us, meaning a patient pays a doctor to help. All too often we give doctors too much power in the relationship and many of them grab that authority much too easily. So instead of empowering their patients, doctors hold on to their own role – being indispensable – instead of being a partner in good mental health.

But let's back up to the diagnosis part.

Being diagnosed is a difficult thing to accept. Some people ignore the diagnosis entirely either because they don't like being labeled, while others may become stubborn, deflect, and claim other people are in the wrong and *should* accept us.

We could say to someone, "I am bipolar. Accept it, or you're a heartless prick and we're done!"

This approach, besides being an unreasonable ultimatum, is not nearly as effective as explaining to a family member, friend, or colleague what we feel and what kind of help and support we might need from them. I find it's ideal to walk them through the specifics when we are clear-headed, and they are most receptive. It helped me to roleplay the scenarios with my therapist.

As a rule, if we don't have a sound reason for why we're telling someone something so private, then maybe think twice about doing it.

If we choose to divulge, imagine how much more helpful it is to say the following:

"I was recently diagnosed with bipolar, which means I'm more prone to depression or hypomania than the average person. I manage this by going to therapy, working out, getting enough sleep, eating healthy foods, and taking meds. But when I get to a place where I am visibly stressed, I will ask you to insist I take a 30-minute coffee break, and if you're free, accompany me."

Then comes a clear request from us to them:

"Is this something you can help me with?"

In contrast, flat out telling someone we are bipolar means little since bipolar is like snowflakes. Two diagnoses may be similar but no two are alike. And to complicate matters, the characteristics of any single diagnosis constantly change form.

I've said the following before to a co-worker, someone I recognized to be a supportive ally:

"Sometimes I experience bouts of anxiety when I work too late at night and have a deadline that I don't think I'll be able to make."

And this:

"When I'm anxious, I tend to get really flustered, make mistakes, and become irritable.

"In anticipation of that, I take Ativan, my as-needed medication, to help me stay grounded, but if this is not enough I might ask you to tell me when I'm getting agitated and insist I go for a short walk, and possibly assure our project team that I'll get back on track to meet the deadline."

Context matters!

Professional Diagnosis

The Diagnostic Statistical Manual (DSM) of the American Psychiatric Association, also known as the Bible for determining any diagnosis, does not have a definitive checklist for diagnosing a mood disorder, only guidelines.

The best evaluation I could find is a brief questionnaire from Dr. Ivan Goldberg, who received the Distinguished

Service Award by the American Psychiatric Association for his extensive contributions in the treatment of mental health disorders.

The responses do not necessarily brand someone bipolar or not bipolar, but they provide great insight:

Am I Bipolar?

Take this quiz to see if you may benefit from further diagnosis and treatment from a mental health professional.

At times I am *much* more talkative or speak *much* faster than usual.

Never	Often
Rarely	Very Often
Sometimes	

There have been times when I was *much* more active or did *many* more things than usual.

Never	Often
Rarely	Very Often
Sometimes	

I get into moods where I may feel *very* speeded up or irritable.

Never	Often
Rarely	Very Often
Sometimes	

There have been times when I have felt both high (elated) and low (depressed) *at the same time*.

Never	Often
Rarely	Very Often
Sometimes	

At times I am *much* more interested in sex than I may usually be.

Never	Often
Rarely	Very Often
Sometimes	

My self-confidence ranges from *great* self-doubt to *equally great* overconfidence.

Never	Often
Rarely	Very Often
Sometimes	

There have been *great* variations in the quantity or quality of my work.

Never	Often
Rarely	Very Often
Sometimes	

For no obvious reason I sometimes have been *very* angry or hostile.

Never	Often
Rarely	Very Often
Sometimes	

Sometimes I am mentally dull and at other times I think *very* creatively.

Never	Often
Rarely	Very Often
Sometimes	

At times I am *greatly* interested in being with people and at other times I just want to be left alone with my thoughts.

Never	Often
Rarely	Very Often
Sometimes	

Sometimes, I have GREAT optimism and at other times EQUALLY GREAT pessimism.

Never	Often
Rarely	Very Often
Sometimes	

Some of the time I show *much* tearfulness and crying and at other times I laugh and joke *excessively*.

Never	Often
Rarely	Very Often
Sometimes	

This test has been based on the bipolar screening question-naire created by the late Dr. Ivan Goldberg, a renowned psy-chiatrist and clinical psycho-pharmacologist.

Source: psycom.net

Bipolar I Versus Bipolar II: Is There Really Anything to Fight About?

It doesn't come up in my groups very often where someone with a more tempered mood disorder like bipolar II is treated less than someone with *real issues*, like bipolar I, borderline, or schizophrenia. But when it does happen, it annoys the hell out of me.

To that I say this: *It's not a competition.*

We all have mental health issues that need support and it takes a team to help one person.

That said, not everyone sees it as I do. For some, it's a badge of honor to have more hospitalizations or more extreme episodes.

There's a fine line between embracing our challenges and excusing our shortcomings.

It's not a competition with anyone else. The perceived competition is a battle within us to improve our well-being.

Buddhist Monks spend their lives on a path of self-improvement, reaching spiritual enlightenment, and self-actualization. Why wouldn't we – none of us being monks, mind you – ever stop choosing to find new strategies and avenues to improve and to support others in need?

Walking on Eggshells

A lot of people with hypomania become euphoric, and describe feeling hypersexual, grandiose, and depending on the level of mania, indestructible.

That's not me!

I get impatient.

Everything pisses me off. My mind starts racing. I want to hit strangers who look at me on the subway ("You have a problem?") or don't look at me at all ("I'm not good enough?").

I get overly principled on social graces.

I get absolutely livid when people take too much room on the sidewalk. I know when I'm really off when I calculate the percentage of room someone should and should not take based on if they are alone, in a couple, couple with kid, couple with dog, where the leash should go, etc.

What else?

Four Types of Bipolar Disorder

Bipolar I Disorder is an illness in which people have experienced one or more episodes of mania. Most people diagnosed with bipolar I will have episodes of both mania and depression, though an episode of depression is not necessary for a diagnosis.

To be diagnosed with bipolar I, a person's manic episodes must last at least seven days or be so severe that hospitalization is required.

Bipolar II Disorder is a subset of bipolar disorder in which people experience depressive episodes shifting back and forth with hypomanic episodes, but never a "full" manic episode.

Cyclothymic Disorder, also called Cyclothymia, is a chronically unstable mood state in which people experience hypomania and mild depression for at least two years. People with cyclothymia may have brief periods of normal mood, but these periods last less than eight weeks.

Finally, Bipolar Disorder "other specified" and "unspecified" is when a person does not meet the criteria for bipolar I, II, or cyclothymia but has still experienced periods of clinically significant abnormal mood elevation.

Source: National Alliance on Mental Illness (NAMI)

Don't get me started on what I might feel when a stranger reclines in my space on a bus or airplane! The flight may say three hours to land, but for me it can feel like an eternity.

My healthy perspective says?

Even with a mood disorder I am fortunate. Bipolar is easier for me to manage because I want to manage it. It's not pleasurable. Also, the journey to improve my mental health has made me more introspective and has deepened my personal relationships.

In contrast, people with bipolar who embrace the mania and ride the highs or believe medication disturbs their creativity are more likely to crash headfirst into a depression.

I'm lucky to have my freedom. For all the dark thoughts I've had and nearly acted on, I could be in prison. Or worse!

So how do I cope?

To start with, I rely on medication. If I don't take my medication, then all bets are off.

Next?

Sleep, exercise, and therapy.

If those don't do the trick?

Practice Mindfulness!

Cops and soldiers use the phrase, "Always vigilant." That's good advice for anyone with a mood disorder. We always need to be aware of our state of mind and how our moods and actions impact other people.

My Meds

I classify *Meds* as an entire menu of mood caretakers, metabolism balancers, impulse managers, healing listeners, action makers, and life sustainers. They include all the categories listed here, along with how each works for me.

Pills

I've taken 200 mg of Lamictal regularly for the past five years – 100 mg before I leave the apartment and 100 mg in the evening (I once took a generic from a different manufacturer and had a severe episode; within 12 hours I called my parents and told them I never want to speak to them again, marched into Verizon and demanded to be taken off my family plan, and would have broken up with my girlfriend if she answered before my parents – same compound of the same med, different lab).

I take 1 mg of Ativan, as needed, when I start to feel anxious. I've been told I could up my meds, but for now I decided to do everything else on my list instead of taking more meds.

Exercise

Two to four times a week, including weightlifting, spin class, elliptical, and yoga.

Meditate

Meditation, especially guided meditation, is helpful for anxiety and to provide clarity. I'm planning to incorporate a regular discipline to help me continue to see the world clearly as it is, not as I'd like it to be.

Therapy

Dialectical/Cognitive Behavioral Therapy for three years, plus group therapy, psychodynamic therapy, and anger management.

Diet and Nutrition

Eat healthily and don't use caffeine unless it's with a full meal. I don't eat much sugar and rarely ever drink alcohol

Medications

With a prescribing doctor, work together to review the options for medication. Different types of bipolar disorder may respond better to a particular type. The side effects can vary between medications and it may take time to discover the best medicine.

Lithium (Lithobid, Eskalith)
Lithium is effective at stabilizing moods and preventing the extreme highs and lows of bipolar disorder. Periodic blood tests are required because lithium can cause thyroid and kidney problems. Common side effects include restlessness, dry mouth, and digestive issues. Lithium levels should be monitored carefully to ensure the best dosage and watch for toxicity.

Lithium is used for continued treatment of bipolar depression and for preventing relapse. There is evidence that lithium can lower the risk of suicide but the FDA has not granted approval for this purpose.

Anticonvulsants
Many medications used to treat seizures are also used as mood stabilizers. They are often recommended for treating bipolar disorder. Common side effects include weight gain, dizziness, and drowsiness. But sometimes, certain anticonvulsants cause more serious problems, such as skin rashes, blood disorders, or liver problems.

Valproic acid and carbamazepine are used to treat mania. These drugs, also used to treat epilepsy, were found to be as effective as lithium for treating acute mania. They may be better than lithium in treating the more complex bipolar subtypes of rapid cycling and dysphoric mania as well as co-morbid substance abuse.

Lamotrigine is used to delay occurrences of bipolar I disorder. Lamotrigine does not have FDA approval for treatment of the acute episodes of depression or mania. Studies of lamotrigine for treatment of acute bipolar depression have produced inconsistent results.

Second-Generation Antipsychotics (SGAs)
SGAs are commonly used to treat the symptoms of bipolar disorder and are often paired with other medications, including mood stabilizers. They are generally used for treating manic or mixed episodes.

SGAs are often prescribed to control acute episodes of mania or depression. Finding the right medication is not an exact science; it is specific to each person. Currently, only quetiapine and the combination of olanzepine and fluoxetine (Symbax) are approved for treating bipolar depression. Regularly check with your doctor and the FDA website, as side effects can change over time.

Standard Antidepressants
Antidepressants present special concerns when used in treating bipolar disorder, as they can trigger mania in some people. A National Institute of Mental Health study showed that taking an antidepressant with a mood stabilizer is no more effective than using a mood stabilizer alone for bipolar I. This is an essential area to review treatment risks and benefits.

Other Treatments

Electroconvulsive Therapy (ECT)
In rare instances, ECT can be considered as an intervention for severe mania or depression. ECT involves transmitting short electrical impulses into the brain. Although ECT is a highly effective treatment for severe depression, mania, or mixed episodes, it is reserved for specific situations and for symptoms that have not responded to other treatments.

Treatment Considerations for Women
Women with bipolar disorder who are of childbearing age or who are considering getting pregnant, need special attention. A complex risk-benefit discussion needs to occur to look at available treatment options. Some medicines can have risks to the developing fetus and to children in breast milk. However, there is also evidence that being off of all medications increases the likelihood of bipolar symptoms, which creates risks to mother and fetus or baby. Planning ahead and getting good information from your health care team based on your individual circumstances improves your chance of a best outcome.

Treatment Considerations for Children
The diagnosis of bipolar disorder in children has been controversial. Before receiving any psychiatric diagnosis, children must have a comprehensive evaluation of their physical and mental health. Children with bipolar disorder may also have other conditions including attention-deficit hyperactivity disorder, early childhood psychosis, posttraumatic stress disorder, learning disabilities, or substance abuse problems. Each of these co-occurring conditions requires a thoughtful and individualized treatment plan. Children with bipolar disorder usually receive psychotherapy and psychosocial interventions before medications are considered.

The identification of a new mental health condition, Disruptive Mood Dysregulation Disorder (DMDD), could affect how bipolar disorder is diagnosed in children. DMDD better describes children who are intensely irritable, have temper tantrums, but do not have classic symptoms of mania. Early evidence suggests children with DMDD do not have an increased risk of developing bipolar disorder as adults, but they may have other co-occurring illnesses like depression.

Source: National Alliance on Mental Illness (NAMI)

(curbed daily habit on August 28, 2010). I don't do recreational drugs.

For those who use marijuana and who say it helps them with anxiety, please be careful. Even if it seems to help – not cause – anxiety, it's impossible to control the exact amount we ingest, the exact strain, and the length of its effects. These are often different and strongly impact other meds in our system. I recommend asking a prescribing doctor about mixing and matching *all* types of drugs.

A Note on Drinking

In December 2010 I wrote in my journal that, "My most extreme behavioral shifts now appear to be addressed, with no more swings from dramatic highs to dramatic lows, like the switch of a light bulb, I find life coming back into my control. Everything is as it ought to be. I am fortunate. My world has options and I choose stability and consistency in everything whenever possible."

My mental health took priority over my social life, so I could have a life.

Relationships

Cultivate and keep friends and family who are supportive but *not* enablers. This is an important distinction. I set up guidelines with my therapist to keep me accountable.

If I yell at my dad, I have to write on loose leaf paper "I will not yell at my dad" 1,000 times and send it to him via express mail within 10 days. He won't talk to me until he receives it. When I become verbally aggressive around my girlfriend, after two direct warnings she'll tell me "Consequence" and I have to shut off all media. This last time I missed the season finale of *Game of Thrones* (which before it aired was a very big deal).

But that's how we learn, by adding people to our lives who hold us to a higher standard that we cannot set and maintain for ourselves.

The other side of the coin: It is tough to acknowledge that certain people are not good for us. Sometimes we may have to choose between friends – even family – and our mental health.

Sleep

Sleep deprivation impacts everyone differently. I lose my ability to think straight. Lack of sleep is an early indicator that I will be easily triggered. If I get back-to-back nights of less than six hours, I become more hypersensitive, intolerant, and often say inappropriate things that only I find amusing.

Writing

Continue my cognitive behavioral therapy exercises where I keep a record of how I feel on a 10-point scale, along with notes on my thoughts, emotions, and plans of action.

This allows me to recognize my cognitive distortions and process my environment more constructively before I act.

Even if we are not following prescribed exercises, we can benefit by keeping a journal to track all sorts of things we are dealing with and trying to understand.

A journal helps prepare for therapy sessions and doctor visits.

Keep to a Routine

When depressed, the last thing I want to do is get up and do anything constructive. My bed is my comfort zone.

I try to plan activities I know I can commit to. I might lie in bed but I'll get my ass up – even if it's at the last minute – to arrive where I plan to be on time, like to a fitness class or to the movies.

When I experience a manic high, I may lift weights or run on a treadmill to level out. Expending energy at the gym has better consequences than punching a hole in the wall (or trying to).

When I get grandiose and feel like nothing can touch me, it's better that I do it within myself and according to my own routine, rather than tell off pedestrians for not giving me an equal percentage on the sidewalk or picking fights on the basketball court while demanding everyone to curl around my perfect screens.

In a depressed state, muscle memory kicks in. Though my mind acts and reacts slowly, it quickly responds favorably to the serotonin.

I know I'll feel better afterwards. That's how I base most of my decisions.

Humor
In *Paradise Lost*, John Milton writes, "The mind can make a heaven out of hell or a hell out of heaven."

Humor enables us to make heaven out of hell. It allows us to examine painful episodes from our past and laugh about them, not to forget, but to help forgive the pain they caused. It empowers us to take back our humanity and regain our better selves from the bipolar beast. It allows me to revisit my missteps and say, "Hell, if I had an employee that behaved like I did, I would have fired him too." Granted,

I would've recognized the signs and sat down with me first, but I'll go into that more in Chapter 5.

I'm not suggesting that humor can allow everyone to go from an aggressive hypomania to a normal baseline, but it helps, especially for those like me who can get overly rigid or principled and need to rely on coping strategies to calm down.

When I am manic, I try to take myself less seriously, because I've witnessed in the hospital what serious really looks like.

Peer Groups
Group allows us to capture a wealth of information from other members with shared life experience. When we're not well, we can listen to other people's experiences and get out of our head for a few hours. When we are doing well, we feel good giving back while also reinforcing our good mental health space.

Miscellaneous and Mindful
There is no shortage of activities that allow us to maintain or strengthen mental health and wellness. Just go on Meetup to find dozens of uplifting activities at low or no cost. I've done group and individual sessions in American Sign Language, theater improvisation, and attended a non-violent communication workshop, all of which challenge me and keep me centered.

Empathy
Sticking to this toolbox is essential for me, but I sometimes get discouraged and might say "fuck it" when I start to

think it is not enough.

If I'm having an off day and someone makes a comment that I should "see someone" or am asked, "Are you off your meds?" I'll take it to heart. I stopped talking to a dear friend over a stupid one-off remark because I took it so personally.

Other times I might just have an off day and tell myself, "I can feel shitty without these meds, why deprive myself of what I enjoy doing if I feel like shit either way?"

This is where empathy comes in to play. Empathy for other people to forgive them for not being perfect, and always for ourselves.

Learning About Empathy

According to *Psychology Today*, "Empathy is the experience of understanding another person's thoughts, feelings, and condition from his or her point of view, rather than from one's own. Empathy facilitates prosocial and/or helping behaviors that come from within, rather than being forced, so that people behave in a more compassionate manner. Although there may be individual differences in empathy based on genetic differences, research suggests it's possible to boost the capacity for empathic understanding."

For those of us with a mood disorder, life's adversities force us to become more self-aware. Our coping strategies allow us to identify with others struggling with a similar condition. With our lived experience, through peer support we can give back to those who are just starting their journey toward mental health and wellness. Talking about ourselves while listening to others, walking them through what works for us and doesn't work, helps to reinforce our good habits and strengthens empathy.

Without the groups I've been in as a participant and facilitator, I wouldn't have a clue how empathy works, let alone its huge value. I wouldn't have a solid foundation about anything mood related. Nothing anyone shares with me would stick, and I'd still be arguing and cursing people out and struggling with most aspects of life. The groups didn't save my life, but they have given it more meaning and purpose.

A Primer on Practicing Empathy

Roman Krznaric, a founding faculty member of The School of Life in London and empathy advisor to organizations including Oxfam and the United Nations, wrote a piece for The Greater Good Science Center at UC Berkeley, called *Six Habits of Highly Empathic People*.

Here are the habits he reports from his research:

Habit 1:
Cultivate curiosity about strangers.

Highly empathic people (HEPs) have an insatiable curiosity about strangers. They will talk to the person sitting next to them on the bus, having retained that natural inquisitiveness we all had as children, but which society is so good at beating out of us.

Curiosity expands our empathy when we talk to people outside our usual social circle, encountering lives and worldviews very different from our own. It is a useful cure for the chronic loneliness afflicting one in three Americans. Set yourself the challenge of having a conversation with one stranger every week.

All it requires is courage.

Habit 2:
Challenge prejudices and discover commonalities.

We all have assumptions about others and use collective labels – "Muslim fundamentalist," or "welfare mom" – that prevent us from appreciating their individuality. Highly empathic people challenge their own preconceptions and prejudices by searching for what they share with people rather than what divides them.

Habit 3:
Try another person's life.

HEPs expand their empathy by gaining direct experience of other people's lives, putting into practice the Native American proverb, "Walk a mile in another man's moccasins before you criticize him."

Habit 4:
Listen hard – and open up.

There are two traits required to become an empathic conversationalist. One is to master the art of radical listening.

HEPs listen hard to others and do all they can to grasp their emotional state and needs, whether it is a friend newly diagnosed with cancer or a spouse who is upset at them for working late yet again.

But listening is never enough.

The second trait is to make ourselves vulnerable. Removing our masks and revealing our feelings is vital for creating strong empathic bonds.

Empathy is a two-way street that is built upon mutual understanding – an exchange of our most important beliefs and experiences.

Habit 5:
Inspire mass action and social change.

We typically assume that empathy happens at the level of individuals, but HEPs understand that empathy can also be a mass phenomenon, bringing fundamental social change.

Just think of the movements against slavery in the 18th and 19th centuries on both sides of the Atlantic. As journalist Adam Hochschild reminds us, "The abolitionists placed their hope not in sacred texts but human empathy," doing all they could to get people to understand the very real suffering on the plantations and slave ships.

Equally, the international trade union movement grew out of empathy between industrial workers united by their shared exploitation. The overwhelming public response to the Asian tsunami of 2004 emerged from a sense of empathic concern for the victims, whose plight was dramatically beamed into our homes on shaky video footage.

Habit 6:
Develop an ambitious imagination.

A final trait of HEPs is that they do far more than empathize with the usual suspects. We tend to believe empathy should be reserved for those living on the social margins or who are suffering. This is necessary, but it is hardly enough. We also need to empathize with people whose beliefs we don't share or who may be "enemies" in some way.

For example, if you are concerned about global warming, it may be worth trying to step into the shoes of oil company executives – understanding their thinking and motivations

– if you want to devise effective strategies to shift them toward developing renewable energy. A little "instrumental empathy" (sometimes known as "impact anthropology") can go a long way.

Source: Roman Krznaric, Six Habits of Highly Empathic People

How Do You Practice Empathy?

Krznaric provides much for us to aspire to, and bipolar or not, we could all do a better job adding more empathy to our toolkits.

Practicing empathy comes easy when we accept that we help ourselves most when we help others.

three

TRIGGERS BEWARE

One of the few advantages of having a mood disorder is that it enables me – or even forces me – to become more aware and empathic. Empathy is knowing what someone else feels, maybe because we've had a similar experience.

Some people embrace bipolar by calling it their superpower, or sixth sense. My optimistic side agrees. Though I also equate that sentiment to Larry David when he talks about having the *good* kind of Hodgkin's disease.

The main drawback of having erratic mood shifts is that after several months of accruing goodwill, we can lose it in an instant. Some people may give us a pass, or benefit of the doubt, but we can't expect everyone to be so magnanimous or patient. Not everyone will empathize.

Sometimes we must accommodate everyone else even when we KNOW we are right, and they're the ones who are nuts!

Radically accepting this truth has been the hardest part of my therapy.

Before and After

I've had issues at work, especially in buttoned-up corporations where appearance and groupthink are the norm and individual quirks are frowned upon.

Since I've had more than my fair share of conflicts, I've come to label these turning points as BI (Before Incident), when I'm considered the best hire the company can make, fast approaching my way to senior management, and AI (After Incident), when in a flash I become a complete wildcard who no longer conforms to the culture and values of the firm and cannot be trusted in front of a client.

This type of swing, triggered by one single incident, can also happen in personal relationships. Once again, we have BI, when I am the ideal boyfriend regarded by exes as "marriage material," invited to happy hours and weddings, on a fast-track to meeting and being accepted by future in-laws. Then comes whatever trigger pops up out of the blue, what I call the AI moment, when I become the proverbial complete f-ing asshole who needs serious help.

Throughout these burn and crash moments, I am still the same person. I try to tell myself these are isolated bad incidents among thousands of good ones, but whoever sees me on my off day often does not see it that way and can lose faith in me for good.

Wherever the incident took place is no longer a safe space – it's *toxic*. I'm convinced everyone is recalibrating my presence, telling me I don't belong.

When it reaches that boiling point, I either leave on my own for self-preservation, or they beat me to it and give me the walking papers.

As often as it's happened it's become prophecy. When I'm at a low I expect to screw up.

Recent Example
Two months before I started writing this book, my managing director asked me to set up a workshop for 30 people. The day of the event I arrived at the venue before seven a.m. on less than five hours of sleep to coordinate. As I was arranging the room with the staff, my co-worker, who was my closest ally, ordered me to grab her a plate.

Whether her demand was in jest or not, my gut reaction, "Do it yourself!" was anything but.

This was not a good look. A six-foot-one, 210-pound minority dude hollering at a five-foot-two, 110-pound white female.

One rash exchange trumped five months of solid performance.

Any of this sound familiar, or relatable?
The question is not whether my co-workers *should* have trusted me to manage logistics for the next special event. They didn't. My team extrapolated the one bad incident to brand me difficult. The managing director questioned every line item even though he had commended me for controlling expenses beforehand. My co-workers stopped smiling at me or asking about my day, even those who had been over to my apartment to watch a pay-per-view sporting event (and it was a really good one, *Tyson Fury vs. Deontay Wilder I*).

At the time I found the results of the fight as unjust as my fate at the company.

A few weeks after my reprimand from Human Resources, I was looking for another job.

It Starts Here

When I got the axe this time, I had a stable support system and stronger mindset. I bounced back as soon as I handed in my MacBook and badge (backpay and one-month severance to fund this book didn't hurt either!). After a lot of therapy and life experience, I can accept when situations like these don't work out. I know what steps to take to recover.

In stark contrast, six years before at age 30, I was not able to rebound from a similar scenario at work where one incident sparked a series of mishaps and hypomanic episodes.

I disregarded the early warning signs. I didn't know what they were. I didn't know how to cope.

(I'm going into detail on this next section because I hear from many people with mood disorders, personality disorders, and generalized anxiety who continue to experience something similar. If you can't relate, then I guarantee people close to you can. They'd be fortunate to know you have a better idea what a mental health decline looks and feels like. It can come from a series of incidents that catastrophize over time. It's often not from one specific life event.)

With a mood disorder, it's difficult to maintain a stable routine that doesn't become overly rigid. Sometimes when we stop doing one thing on our lengthy checklist, we blame ourselves for our shortcoming. If that feeling of failure becomes too discouraging then we're prone to stop everything else on our list.

Finding a sustainable routine is key!

In May 2012, I took my spotty work history and used it to my advantage. I landed a job at a global management consultancy. Basically, the company advises clients on how to improve their processes and procedures, and structures teams to deliver on management's strategy. Each phase of a project goes on for somewhere between three to six months.

I saw myself as a sort of guerilla fighter. I got in, did an effective job, got out, and then moved on without getting too attached to the work or the people.

Rambo without the headband.

If I had an off-day I would tell myself I wouldn't be stuck with one client or team forever.

I joined the financial services group where my Wharton degree from eight years prior still meant something. My ultimate goal was to work on two successful projects before moving to Los Angeles to fulfill my lifelong goal – to work in the media and entertainment capital of the world – *Tinseltown*!

I excelled on the first project. The subject matter was in my wheelhouse – helping an investment firm grow from $25 billion assets under management (AUM) to $50 billion. I had enough experience supporting hedge funds with their infrastructure that the work was second nature. The project team and some of the managers deferred to my expertise.

It went well but it wasn't all great. Some days I felt super-competent and perfectly utilized one minute, but then I'd get a small critique from a co-worker and would be a complete mess the next.

Fortunately, my immediate manager tolerated my off days. She took me out of the office when she sensed my frustrations. She gave me all the time I needed.

I cannot express how important it is to have a supportive ally at work. When you do find one, be thankful, treasure that person, and find whatever opportunities you can to reciprocate.

I did all I could to help her, to make her look good. I put in time after hours and on weekends. She, in turn, coached me before my meetings with the client. We became a solid duo and delivered great work.

The consultancy gave us a performance evaluation after each project, grading us on a scale of 1 (nice knowing you) to 5 (walks on water). The score is meant to be objective, but when "works well with others" is factored in it becomes a bit biased. Favoritism, politicking, and ass-kissing are a few reasons people decide to leave prematurely.

Anyway, I crushed that first project, receiving one 3, two 4s, and a 5, which is rare. As a senior associate, I was on the senior partners' radar and was fast-tracking to management.

Watch out Disneyland, here I come!

Shit Happens

From there, I moved to another project an hour from my parents' house outside Philadelphia. Once again, the subject matter was in my sweet spot – regulatory reporting for investment firms.

The work addressed regulations imposed by Obama's financial advisors to pre-empt another financial crisis like we had in 2008 (for those in the industry, Form PF). At its core, the work kept partners and engagement managers rich, and minions like me busy. But it paid well enough and allowed me to see my folks each week for a good old-fashioned Sunday Chinese dinner – *the reform Jew staple!*

The project wasn't Monday to Thursday with the client, as promised when I joined. We had to spend all day onsite on Friday too. This meant taking a train Sunday afternoon from New York City to Philly, staying at my parents' house Sunday night, and then taking a train and a bus to the client site on Monday by nine a.m.

I worked most of the day in my cubicle. The only place within walking distance was a WaWa market across the mini-highway. For those who haven't experienced greatness, in the Philly area WaWa is considered a religious experience, but with few other options even I couldn't eat their six-inch hoagies every day for lunch.

I had two options for housing: Stay at a local bed-and-breakfast where I would be the youngest occupant by at least 20 years, or with my co-workers in a hotel five miles down the road where I would have to depend on their commuting schedule and forced to endure their bro-ish humor.

I couldn't make my own schedule work, so how could I conform to theirs too?

I lost my weekly therapist. I didn't have my support group. Even my gym schedule fell apart. Basically, my whole support system – other than my parents' sympathy – completely crumbled.

Know Your Comfort Zone. Then Expand It.

Here is an image I have worked on since my behavioral therapist told me I needed strategies to be more comfortable outside my limited comfort zone:

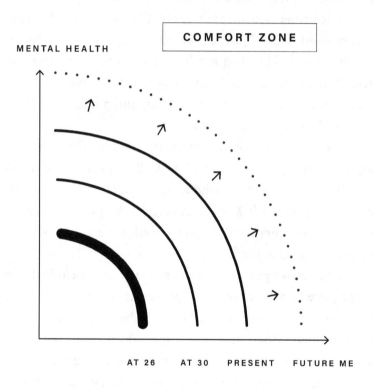

I worked with her to recognize when I was out of my element and to find better ways to react under stress. Over several months she helped arm me with tools to grow my toolkit.

But at this time, at 30, I still had a very small comfort zone: my apartment (when it was clean), my work (as long as I was performing), a movie theater (as long as no one around me was talking or texting), my regular vacation spot (as long as it was sunny), my parents' home (when my brother wasn't there), the gym (when there were no couples working out together), and playing pickup basketball (as long as my teammates ran an efficient motion offense).

When someone talked or texted in a movie, when my brother shut me down by dominating a discussion, when my teammates poorly emulated Allen Iverson and turned the ball over instead of playing as a team, or when I saw something as innocuous as a handful of couples toasting like they were royalty at their *boozy brunch* when I was sitting alone, I got triggered and no longer felt at ease.

Back to the grind.

Grasping Straws

When I felt uneasy, most mornings my half-baked strategy was to hide in my cubicle away from everyone, focus on my work, and limit interactions to instant messenger.

Unfortunately, even when it was 20 degrees outside, the vent above me pumped cold air like clockwork at 11 a.m. and again at 2:30 p.m. It was the only thing I could rely on.

Hibernating there was a bad strategy.

Quick recap: I was stuck in the middle of nowhere with no support. I had to coordinate my lunches around other people's schedule. I couldn't walk anywhere to de-stress. I didn't have access to my support groups. I was forced to be around people who drank at night and gave me a hard time for being anti-social. There was only one person in the area on the OK Cupid dating site (pre- Tinder, Bumble) who I met the third week – unsuccessfully.

A string of inconveniences for most. For me this was a looming disaster.

One incredibly anxious morning in January 2013, just five weeks into the 16-week project, I buried my head in my arms, put my headphones on, and pleaded with myself to get through the day.

To be cute, my co-worker poked me in the rib to give me a fist bump. In response, I impulsively smacked his hand as hard as I could.

At least half the side of the office stopped, got up, and turned around to figure out what the hell that was. I quickly turned my chair around and stared at my monitor, praying I could take back the last five seconds of my life.

Reality set in fast. I knew immediately I wouldn't survive my mistake. The guy I smacked was charismatic and well-liked.

I didn't go to lunch that day. I didn't leave my cubicle. I didn't need anyone to see me crying and shaking and shivering.

I regained my faculties hours later when I saw the co-worker that I hit with our manager walking back from lunch, laughing, enjoying life and letting me know he was untouchable.

When I finally unlocked my PC, I received emails from my counselor, engagement manager, financial services partner, and someone in human resources with a mishmash of senders and CCs, asking me what the hell had happened.

They all told me the same thing.

Respond ASAP!

Before I could, I was generously escorted by the manager to meet in the client's private office that he must have reserved before their *informative* lunch. He sat across from me leaning back in his chair with his legs crossed, his hair parted like a dick parts his hair, checking his Blackberry while he told me I was in the wrong. He notified my counselor, the partner, and apparently everyone else with the company's domain.

He didn't let me say a word.

I shouldn't have hit my co-worker. I should've realized that I was in a place where something as harmless as being poked in the ribs would provoke such a response. At least that's what I told my parents, my therapists, my managers, and everyone else who asked.

He deserved worse. I despised them all.

I hated how white people stuck together and treated people that look like me – and not like them – like I'm subhuman, like I'm only here to do their bidding as long as it wasn't too inconvenient. I hated the injustice cronyism was to people like me. I hated these people for sabotaging my future.

From then on, I vented to anyone who would listen that the world was fucked, which I tried to limit to my parents after work and during the day waiting in line for my daily sub and SunChips, but most often to the one guy who felt the project "wasn't for him but that another company where he wouldn't have to travel as much might be a better fit."

Whatever! Get an inch, take a mile.

I was reprimanded. I was branded a miscreant. I stopped going to lunch with them and didn't go to mandatory outings. I stayed on the project though, since I was doing most of my work with the client and they didn't know about the exchange.

I was a toxic employee and had a lot of disturbing thoughts I couldn't shake. I was:

Troubled.

Manic.

Depressed.

A Victim.

The formal warning went on my record, meaning I could say adios to my promotion. I had to disclose to Human Resources why I needed *special accommodations.*

Coming from a company that gets perpetually ranked in the Top 100 companies to work for, I had hoped this would come with, "I'm glad to help," or "I'm sorry you have to live like this."

Nope!

I was chastised for not telling them earlier.

I learned the hard way that Human Resources is set up to protect a company, not the individual.

I spent $300 a session with my new weekend therapist to help me draft my reasonable accommodations.

Human Resources' response:

"Michael, I understand you need help with lighting and separate seat arrangements so you're not under a cooling duct in the middle of winter, but we're a consultancy and we can't ask the client for these special privileges."

A reasonable response. My reaction:

"The Americans with Disabilities Act and HR can go fuck themselves!"

This is especially true since it disincentivizes hiring full-time employees; instead, it encourages exploiting exposable freelance consultants who get promised to be brought on full-time, only to be used and abused and discarded at-will while skirting rules that the legislation prescribes to protect.

Rant over. Back to my cubicle.

Shortly after, I added medication to curb my aggression – Seroquel – and upped my Lamictal, just so I could keep my head down, do my work, and cope with being an outcast 50 hours a week.

I spoke with co-workers only when I absolutely had to. Instead, I worked extra hours with the client. I killed myself in the gym and gorged on food and Seroquel to fall asleep.

I continued to make mistake after mistake.

I sent an email directly to the client's HR department since my company failed to accommodate me when the cooling vent now caused me to break out in hives. The client forwarded my request with a nasty email to my company. I caught hell from the senior manager.

Now she was my biggest trigger.

I physically moved my computer to the other side of the office – desktop, not laptop – without asking permission, which is when the client caught on.

Self-preservation trumped good judgment.

Things got worse. There was the stormy Friday evening when the engagement partner insisted on driving me to the station. On the way, he made a wrong turn, got caught in traffic for over an hour while blaming me. This privileged prick, driving an $80,000 Benz, blaming me for making him late for the weekend to his three-million-dollar house. This is the same guy who when he last visited us, bragged about how clever he was for screwing people out of pooled bonuses by paying them first, so that he could keep the lion's share for himself.

In case you missed it, I have an issue being slighted by elitist white men. It's better now, but the wounds might be too deep to ever go away.

I was on the brink. I nearly got out of the car in the middle of the highway. Instead, I called my father for direction (and directions) because I was too gone to know where to go. My father told me to ask the partner to drop me off anywhere and he'd pick me up.

The initial destination was 30th Street Station, back to New York City for another 1.5 days – and therapy session – before returning to my parents Sunday evening and then back to the toxic office Monday morning. We went to Trenton instead. I spent the weekend comatose at my parents' house under heavy watch.

When the engagement partner dropped me off in

Trenton, he told me I needed to do a better job communicating. He didn't say anything of substance to me for the rest of the project.

In the end, he gave me a 2 rating for people skills with a blisteringly poor review. The managers confirmed the 2 with a slightly more intelligible reason citing the on-site incidents, not the car ride or refusing to break bread with him to conclude the project.

I received a 4 for *Performance* since the client praised my work.

But it was the 2 for *People* that confirmed my doneness at the consultancy.

The project finally ended in March 2013.

More Shit Happens

I made a feeble attempt to move from financial services to media and entertainment.

The NYC partner in media read my chilling and conflicting work history and couldn't reconcile how someone could be so polar opposite.

Never has she seen something so inconsistent in her 15 years!

She took me on for a two-week trial period because she was a *Great* Samaritan, not to appease HR and Legal and gain points with the financial services' partner!

As much as I could at the time, I tried to stay positive and bond with the new crew.

It was a farce and I didn't stand a chance.

I was barely hanging on. My friend from group with

borderline personality was just hospitalized again. I got kicked out of Equinox, my sanctuary for six years.

The last thing I wanted to hear was their First World problems.

The *rising star* from Williams College was conflicted because she had two weddings to attend and couldn't decide which to go to and what dress to wear.

The others were full of similar superficial bullshit.

The six-foot-four senior manager with his perfect blond hair and blue eyes – and blue-blazer with the family crest that resembled the Mayflower – told us he struggled to come to terms with his future in-laws. He hadn't yet received their blessing to marry their perfect daughter because he liked to yacht in his downtime and this would conflict with her family vacations.

I stopped laughing when I realized he was serious. They didn't appreciate my reaction.

What was I supposed to say when it was my turn?

I had been invited to one wedding over the past five years. The only time I went boating it was a canoe that my father flipped over. I live on sarcasm; most WASPs I went to school with, also known as White Anglo-Saxon Protestants (for those WASPs who don't know who they are), do not.

As the black sheep in the crowd, I did my tasks as directed but didn't fit in.

Needless to say, Captain Gilligan and his faithful crew wouldn't let me stay aboard their ship for long.

In April 2013, I moved back to financial services for an internal – not client-facing – project.

Out of increasing desperation, I spent evenings lining up calls with West Coast partners in media.

Most meetings didn't go anywhere. I received the occasional, "It seems like you're really passionate, I'll keep you in mind," or "We have nothing available now but you should reach out to these people instead." I realized there was only so much I could do over the phone.

I had banked on one crucial in-person meeting with the West Coast engagement partner for Disney, which took me three weeks to schedule through his personal assistant. I waited outside his office for 20 minutes after our scheduled meeting time. He came out in a beautifully-cut dark blue, custom-made suit. While sifting through his Blackberry he blew me off without even looking up to acknowledge me.

"I can't talk now; I'm going to miss my flight."

He walked right past me. I knew my transfer was not gonna happen.

Three weeks later I was assigned to a project in Los Angeles, but not for a film gig. I was forced to work on the worst bullshit project the company could assign someone to – anti-money-laundering (AML) regulatory filing.

If this is punishment for not fitting in; mission accomplished. Put out to legal pasture. All because someone infiltrated my space on an off day and I couldn't cope.

Can You Say Cognitive Distortion?

According to John M. Grohol, PsyD, "Cognitive distortions are simply ways that our mind convinces us of something that isn't really true. These inaccurate thoughts are usually used to reinforce negative thinking or emotions – telling ourselves things that sound rational and accurate, but really only serve to keep us feeling bad about ourselves."

We can make a small mistake at work and process "I should quit," or see a co-worker as either a great ally who we would take a bullet for, or the bane of our existence.

Being bipolar magnifies the negativity and makes us more susceptible to cognitive distortion.

15 Common Cognitive Distortions

In 1976, psychologist Aaron Beck first proposed the theory behind cognitive distortions. In the 1980s, David Burns was responsible for popularizing it with common names and examples for the distortions.

1. Mental Filtering

Magnifying negative details and filtering out the positives. For example, getting a 99 on a test and dwelling on the 1 you missed.

2. Polarized Thinking (or "Black and White" Thinking)

We're either perfect or a complete and abject failure. Seeing the world as either/or, with no shades of gray or middle ground.

3. Overgeneralization

Reaching a conclusion based on a single incident or piece of evidence. If something bad happens just once, they expect it to happen over and over again. For me, getting fired and believing I will never land a stable job again.

4. Jumping to Conclusions

Knowing what another person is feeling or thinking and exactly why they act the way they do. For example, giving advice after hearing one or two snippets of someone's life story.

5. Catastrophizing

Expecting disaster to strike. A person hears about a problem and uses *what if* questions ("What if tragedy strikes?" or "What if it happens to me?") to imagine the absolute worst occurring.

6. Personalization

Believing that everything others do or say is some kind of direct, personal reaction to them. They literally take everything personally, even when something is not meant in that way. A person who experiences this kind of thinking will also compare themselves to others. A person engaging in personalization may also see themselves as the cause of some unhealthy external event that they were not responsible for.

7. Control Fallacies

If we feel *externally controlled*, we see ourselves as a helpless victim of fate. For *internal control*, we assume responsibility for the pain and happiness of everyone around us.

8. Fallacy of Fairness

Feeling resentful because we think we know what is fair, but other people won't agree. People who go through life applying a measuring stick against every situation, judging its "fairness," will often feel resentful, angry, and even hopeless because of it.

9. Blaming

Holding other people responsible for their emotional pain. They may also take the opposite track and instead blame themselves for every problem, even those clearly outside their own control.

10. Shoulds

"Should" statements appear as a list of ironclad rules about how every person should behave. People who break the rules make a person following these "should" statements angry. They also feel guilty when they violate their own rules. A person may often believe they are trying to motivate themselves with shoulds and shouldn'ts, as if they have to be punished before they can do anything.

11. Emotional Reasoning

Whatever a person is feeling is believed to be true automatically and unconditionally. A person's emotions take over their thinking entirely, blotting out all rationality and logic. Saying "if I feel that way, it must be true."

12. Fallacy of Change

Expecting that other people will change to suit them if they just pressure or cajole them enough. A person needs to change people because their hopes for success and happiness seem to depend entirely on them. This distortion is often found in thinking around relationships.

13. Global Labeling ("Mislabeling")

Generalizing one or two qualities into a negative global

judgment about themselves or another person. Instead of describing an error in context of a specific situation, a person will attach an unhealthy universal label to themselves or others.

14. *Always Being Right*

Continually putting other people on trial to prove that their own opinions and actions are the absolute correct ones. To a person engaging in "always being right," being wrong is unthinkable. Being right often is more important than the feelings of others around a person who engages in this cognitive distortion, even loved ones.

15. *Heaven's Reward Fallacy*

False belief that a person's sacrifice and self-denial will eventually pay off, as if some global force is keeping score. This is a riff on the fallacy of fairness, because in a fair world, the people who work the hardest will get the largest reward. A person who sacrifices and works hard but doesn't experience the expected payoff will usually feel bitter when the reward doesn't come.

Source: PsychCentral.com, John M. Grohol, Psy.D., January 2019

Addressing Your Distortions

It's not easy to mitigate our cognitive distortions. But there are ways to cut down the learning curve. The first step is to *recognize* when we are thinking irrationally.

When I started behavioral therapy, my therapist had me keep a mood-tracking diary for six months so we could understand my triggers. I used a scale of 1 to 10 (depressed to euphoric); the date and time; and my stream of conscious thoughts, emotions ascribed to the thoughts, and how I often reacted. The patterns jumped out at me.

Here Grohol gives his ten-step approach to manage cognitive distortions:

1. Identify your cognitive distortion: Which of the 15 distortions are causing your irrational thinking?

2. Examine evidence: Remove yourself from the situation and try to separate fiction (your opinion stemming from bias) from fact.

3. Double standard method: Talk to yourself like you would a friend or family member in need, with kindness and compassion.

4. Thinking in shades of gray: When you're thinking in extremes, tell yourself that there *is* a middle ground.

5. Experimental method: Test your hypothesis to determine if your irrational thinking is legit.

6. Survey method: Seek the opinions of others to determine if your thoughts and attitudes are realistic.

7. Semantic method: Remove judgmental statements, such as "should," with something more positive such as "wouldn't it be nice..."

8. Definitions: Question negative labels, such as "I'm a failure." What does it mean? Relative to who, or what, or how can I be a failure when I have succeeded in the past?

9. Re-attribution: Take responsibility when warranted.

Don't point the finger at yourself to take the blame for someone else's mistake or a systemic issue.

10. Cost-benefit analysis: If you think the advantages of believing a thought outweigh the disadvantages, then you'll find it easier to talk back and refute your original irrational belief.

Identifying Triggers and Managing Your Moods

If I sprain my ankle playing basketball, I immediately recognize the throbbing pain. I see my ankle swell and feel physical anguish. If I don't "ice, rest, and Advil," the pain worsens, and I'm forced to stop playing.

In contrast, when I am emotionally triggered, I often don't process it immediately. I need other people to tell me I'm talking louder than usual and becoming irritable and argumentative. When the mental anguish increases, I'm more likely to keep going until I have an episode.

Since I do not have a very patient and forgiving network or a PR team like Russell Crowe's in his heyday, I cannot depend on other people to turn a blind eye when I explode. I need to take whenever steps necessary to get back to a healthier mindset.

The ten-step approach is good, but it's hard to employ in the moment, on the spot, like I failed to do in my two work interactions.

In hindsight, it might have helped to visualize my mood shifts like we can with a physical injury.

I equate my mood stability to how I'm able to manage daily triggers. When I am doing well, I can tolerate daily noise. When I am *not* doing well, I cannot tolerate nearly as much, and I process and address most events poorly.

It's important to recognize when our moods are not in sync with everyday events.

Here are a few scenarios:

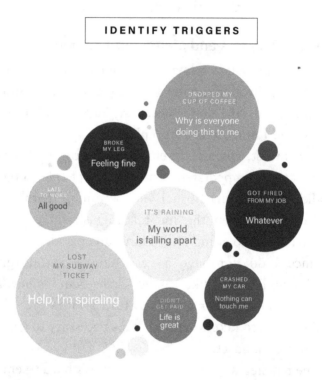

IDENTIFY TRIGGERS

DROPPED MY
CUP OF COFFEE
Why is everyone
doing this to me

BROKE
MY LEG
Feeling fine

LATE
TO WORK
All good

GOT FIRED
FROM MY JOB
Whatever

IT'S RAINING
My world
is falling apart

LOST
MY SUBWAY
TICKET
Help, I'm spiraling

DIDN'T
GET PAID
Life is
great

CRASHED
MY CAR
Nothing can
touch me

When I was younger, the smallest annoyance would set me off. Now, with the work I've put in, it usually takes something more monumental to trigger me into an emotional state. But I'm still not where I want to be – in a place where I can tolerate triggers that continue to affect me; and when

I'm triggered, I don't have to work so hard to cope.

We can be mildly triggered for a long period of time (seated behind someone reclining on an intercontinental flight), massively triggered for a short amount of time (feeling the need to smack a co-worker), or many scenarios in between.

When we get triggered and don't have any effective strategies such as taking an opposite action, going for a walk, working out, listening to a favorite song, talking to a friend, or taking an as-needed medication, then we might be left hoping for the best which doesn't work because of how easy it is to lose sight of what our baseline looks and feels like.

We're able to manage our range of emotions better when we learn to monitor our daily triggers.

The goal is to increase our tolerance levels so we don't get triggered as easily, and when we do, we have an action plan in our back pocket ready to be utilized so that triggers don't lead to episodes.

Employ Effective Strategies When You are Triggered

When we are triggered, our defense drops. It's like getting hit by an asteroid field (slew of triggers in different shapes coming at us from every direction). Those speeding chunks of energy coming at us may be represented by an influx of emails just before we're about to give a presentation, by someone bumping into us on the subway and not apologizing, seeing a couple show public displays of affection after we've been dumped, by a girl who stopped returning our Tinder messages, or by getting a bad review from a manager.

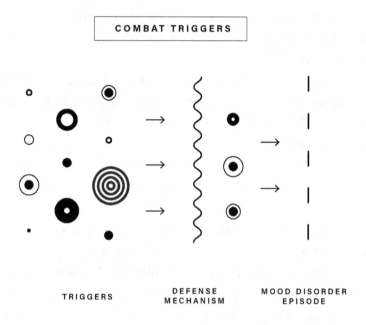

The stronger our tolerance levels – or defense mechanism – the less likely any of the asteroids will penetrate our mental health stability.

When we are not practicing self-care – like when we forego sleep, haven't worked out in several days, or have been working too many hours – our defense weakens and we're more likely to have an episode.

We don't want triggers to make us feel any more manic or depressed, and we definitely don't want to act irrationally when our mental health is jeopardized.

Persona Non Grata

I was 24 years old when I first attempted to work in the movie business. On an impulse, I quit my job and worked as an unpaid line producer (fancy name for bookkeeper) for a small independent project. I spent three weeks with 12 other people sleeping five hours a night on air mattresses in a one-story house in Piscataway, New Jersey, in 100-degree temperatures.

It was the greatest job I ever had, but "living the dream" didn't pay the bills.

Fast forward to June 2013.

I thought I was lucky being assigned to work in Los Angeles. Movie town! This was going to be my redemption with swimming pools and movie stars, just like the Beverly Hillbillies. Instead, I was stuck filing reports for an anti-money-laundering project.

Bright lights, big city? *Fuhgeddaboudit!*

I tried to convince myself this project would work. I plunged myself into the assignment. I did my research. I read books and articles and prepared everything I could in advance. I was going to be a subject matter expert before I joined the team.

When I got to the client site, a gorgeous complex in L.A., I was introduced to the senior manager, a clone of the self-entitled senior manager in New York.

The *trailblazer* conducted himself as if he had invented the concept of pre-empting financial crimes. In his spare time, as he put it, he golfed with Senator Chris Dodd and Congressman Barney Frank who spearheaded the nation's federal regulatory laws in the aftermath of the financial crisis.

With a smug expression, he lined up our team in his private office like the von Trapp family, in order of irrelevance. I stood next to a junior analyst, who looked extremely junior even for a junior analyst. I was at least five years older than everyone else.

We were instructed to tell him in 30 seconds, preferably less, who we are and how we were going to make this project build a better rapport with his client.

Our role was to document wire transfers that exceed $5,000, indicate who sent it and received it, if either had a criminal record, were a PEP (Politically Exposed Person), and which banks were in the transaction. Suspicious wires went to government agencies who we were told usually did nothing with the report.

To my 22-year-old co-workers fresh out of undergrad, this was a stress-free gig in paradise. For me, this was a painful reminder about how little I'd accomplished.

I was the notorious 31-year-old who had not been promoted to manager. Instead, I was stuck taking orders from children posing as adults who talked to me like I was a toddler.

This is what I had accomplished in life:

My New Timeline: The Cliff Notes Version

Public school to top private school. ✔

Top private school to top college. ✔

Top college to full-time job. ✔

Entry level to senior level. ✔

Senior level corporate to career in film where I can excel and feel validated. **NO.**

Career in film delayed. ✔

Back to entry level. ✔

My whole life (all the shit I've put up with and fought through) was supposed to be a means to an end. I rose to one of the top management consultancies after years of shoveling shit. Now here I was, all because of one asshole who was now promoted to run his own team.

Deflecting. ✔

Blaming. ✔

Scathing. ✔

Here is a blow-by-blow account of what happens to someone stuck in a hypomanic episode:

The Incident

On January 18, 2013 after my first day of work, I dined with a co-worker. I got back to the hotel at 10:30 p.m. I couldn't sleep. I needed to burn off stress from working 10 hours straight in a 250 square-foot office with 12 computers and so many anxiety-inducing millennials.

I decided to go for a run. I passed the Disney movie studio. I began to break down.

Why was I on the outside and not working on the inside of that studio?

I kept running, this time past Warner Brothers where I felt even more irrelevant.

No one gives a shit about me. Everyone is in my way. I hate the world. These monuments were placed here to insult me!

I had no idea how hard or far I ran but it was too dark and I was too exhausted to keep going.

Walking back to the hotel, I thought about all the times I had acted out. Did acting out ever help me? My screaming. My cursing at close relatives who are now in Philly sound asleep. Should I wake them?

Out of control.

I'd been fired for acting out. I'd lost gym memberships for acting out. I'd had countless breakups for acting out. I'd lost all my friends from high school and college for acting out. I'd been cast aside where I currently was for acting out.

I'm stronger than this, for sure. I'll make the most of this project.

I kept running.

Day Two

A young woman with minimal work experience got assigned to supervise my work. She is perfectly thin with perfect posture.

I asked the manager a question about the filing process. Our newest superstar jumped right in to make herself look good – the unwritten formula for success which she also picked up quicker than most – at my expense. The manager responded with a smile to validate her teaching prowess from Day One, and her excellent delegation skills.

I can't do this right, either! And, I didn't catch a word of that. Fuck it, I'll figure it out myself.

I wanted to break her prideful posture like a twig.

Chill! Not!

A man-child barged into our sweatshop to invite us out to watch the NBA Finals, Game 6, so we could celebrate his 25th birthday. We were three hours behind on the West Coast, which reminded me that I would miss the first half of the game.

Dammit!

Before he left, he told us – with a real shit-ass smile – to get back to work, and then waddled off in his oversized crappy suit.

I want to smash your skull in and then throw your dying corpse off the 41st floor. Why is my right hand shaking?!

Those unathletic know-it-alls talked about the basket-ball game for the next 10 minutes. They knew nothing about basketball but had strong convictions. They were so sure about everything in the world and had barely lived in it. They didn't ask my opinion about anything. I was a nobody to them.

Shut your fucking mouths! Shut. The fuck. Up!!

Pull Back

I had been there two days. They'd been there several months. I kept mute. I knew that if I talked, things would get bad quickly.

In popped one of those high-maintenance types, three hours late in her three-inch pumps. My blood pressure spiked 20 points. I hated that bitch. After three seconds, I knew her life story. We stood in unison to greet her. She accepted us the way a princess greets her subjects. An honor and a privilege? You motherfucking bitch....

She went around the room to regale us with her flight delays that magically worked out for the best when she got upgraded (of course) while the minions waited their turn to say stupid shit to pique her interest.

Stay cool, Michael. I must not react.

But bad thoughts flooded my brain. Why was I not working in film? I'd put in the time. I'd done everything I could to be placed on the Disney project – it's right next door!

I've been pushed aside. I've been forgotten.

Time for lunch, an equal playing field. I couldn't screw up lunch. Time to enjoy the promenade on an 80-degree day. Time to find out if L.A. was right for me. It's the reason I'm here. A co-worker provided great insight. West Hollywood you say? I'll look into Brentwood.

Lunch was going well. The tide was turning.

Wrong!

The queen arrived fashionably late. Her tight blouse

hugged her perfectly as if she'd be going straight from work to a photo shoot.

The client senior managers who had been ignoring us were now eyeing her in admiration. She adjusted her perfect posture, which they noticed. She unleashed her thousand-dollar purse and parked it on the table where its jewels glared right into my eyes.

The gray-haired, self-righteous smug managing director took another long second to undress this woman with his eyes before asking her to discuss her weekend.

I don't give a shit that you went to the beach. That you dyed your hair. That your life is perfect!

I zoned out to turn my attention back to my new insightful co-worker. He, like the rest of the lemmings, was now wrapped around this bitch's perfectly manicured finger. He ignored my next question.

I looked up and counted to 10.

I hated this fucking bitch. People like this ignored me all through grade school and still acted like they knew how the fucking world works because it operated so perfectly in their favor, as if they knew best and were entitled to their benefits.

I hate them all.

Spinning Out

Everyone was still eating. I had my co-worker's attention again, discussing the Academy Award-nominated films that were just getting released to video.

This same bitch cut me off to declare that *Zero Dark Thirty* was an awful film.

I can't bottle this. I've bottled enough for one morning. For a lifetime.

"What was your problem with it?" I asked.

"It was awful. There was no score and there was no suspense building up to capturing Obama bin Laden. It was nothing like *The Rock*."

It's O-s-ama bin Laden, for Christ's sake. I bit my tongue. Everyone stopped eating and responded in unison:

"Yeah, you're right. Now that was a great movie."

I muttered, "Michael Bay! Michael fucking Bay!"

My muttering got progressively louder and audible. I wanted to scream at her, "You are a fucking moron!" I was shaking and my body had gone cold. I needed to say something.

I need to leave.

I stormed off with half my lunch uneaten.

I Need, I Need

No one who tells me what to do in this world can find this fucking shit interesting. Why can't I work on a project I know I'll love? Something I know resonates with me, validates me. It's because of stupid fucks like her, under-qualified to open their mouths unless it flatters their ego.

Can anyone blame me for wanting to remove myself from this fucked-up world, or how it sometimes makes me feel and behave?

I hate myself when I get like this.

Ballin'!

When we got back to the office, my 20-year-old manager told us, while texting, that if we filed enough reports we could leave 30 minutes early to catch most of the basketball game.

Thanks for your permission, kid!!

We rushed to the local sports bar after work. The second half just started. I quickly fell back into my comfort zone. It's basketball.

I'm home.

I made brilliant observations on the defensive adjustments by both coaches since games four and five, but my colorful gems fell on deaf ears. They didn't know shit about basketball. My new co-worker kept rooting for the Heats. It's the fucking *Heat*, I told him (in my head, not out loud), not the Heats, you dumb bastard.

Stop pretending you know this shit!

Only 10.3 seconds remained in the third quarter. Soon we'd be sitting instead of standing in the bar area to comfortably watch the fourth quarter, ordering perfectly good bar food on the company's dime.

One redneck asshole in a backward hat who didn't say a word about the game told me I'm blocking his view. He demanded that I move so he could watch the game. All I had to do was move. So, of course, I escalated.

"You're not watching this," I told him. "You're talking the entire time. Go back to your discussion and I'll stand where the fuck I've been for the past twenty minutes."

Here come the beer muscles.

His friend realized I was bigger than him, but I was with two idiots who obviously wouldn't do shit. He got up to curse me out, to intimidate me so he could feel tough in front of his woman.

I didn't take the bait. I shut off. My whole body shook. I knew that I couldn't act on this. I knew where it would lead. That made me shut down and tear up, as I often do when I can't express myself.

Instead, I mumbled incoherently. I did this instead of retaliating with threats or even worse, with violence. I wouldn't succumb to a bar fight.

Make this go away.

Opposite Action!

I had a glass of Diet Coke in my right hand. I quit drinking three years ago to keep me from getting into situations I can't control. Now I was thinking, what the fuck for? Why? I could break my glass over this guy's head and slit the other one's throat in seconds.

My mind calculated how I would execute the attack. It would be perfect. But I'd made promises to my family and to myself.

I rushed to the hostess to see if she could intervene.

Rescue me.

I didn't use those exact words, but that's what I needed, someone to help me from hurting myself when I hurt this asshole. She broke up the dick-measuring discussion and put us in separate seats away from the bar, close to another TV.

I was manic during the entire fourth quarter. I felt

hateful. I was bitter that the Spurs blew the lead and most likely the entire series. I was pissed off that LeBron's arrogance was on full display.

Why am I taking this so personally?

I couldn't shake the burning desire to confront my new bar friends. I bottled it all up. Besides, I wasn't Antonio Banderas or Patrick Swayze. It's not my thing to get into bar fights.

The game was hugely disappointing, but I didn't kill anyone or get myself thrown in prison, so this could be considered a win.

The next morning my mania and blood pressure were on display. I got in to work 30 minutes early to explain to the project manager that I have anxiety and need to sit away from my co-workers. I knew the process and could manage on my own. With my aggressive tone she knew better than to say no.

My Bubble

I was moved to a cubicle exposed to client managers and consultants, all with more responsibility than I had. Most were younger than me. Some discussed golf. They all had an opinion on that sport, but it's not something I could chime in on because it hadn't been mainstreamed yet to include too many blacks or Jews.

Fuck golf. And fuck you.

I went completely unnoticed. Completely ignored. Completely left alone to do one fucking task over and over. I was told I needed to do this 45 hours each week for six months; fly home on Friday and back by Monday morning. So far, it's only been two days and two hours.

This is a bullshit project to maintain the company's lifeblood – *file and bill, file and bill, file and bill* – which I must do since my billing utilization went to hell after my last client-facing project.

Eight years after graduating from what many call the best business school in the world, I was watching most of my peers rise up the ranks to senior management positions. I'd been overlooked, condescended to, and marginalized.

What's the big deal about a mood disorder when you're having so much fun?

Hilarious

If there is a God, He has a sense of humor. Showing me the first day there what I could have had and feeding me shit instead.

Neglected. Irrelevant. Why am I even alive?

On the third day of a six-month project in this sunny California paradise, I acted purely out of self-preservation when I dragged myself to Cedars-Sinai, Los Angeles' world-renowned hospital, to find solace. I ended up on a gurney in a psych ward in Alhambra.

Will this decision help me find any comfort?

Act and React

I went into the hospital questioning why I was alive, and then spent six hours on a flight home asking myself, "What do I do now?"

I have a mood disorder. It doesn't define me. It won't hold me back. I won't let it be a crutch.

I chose to put more work into therapy, add disciplines and widen my life experience, so the same triggers don't hit me nearly as hard as before. I will see them coming and know how to manage them.

Over time, I stopped having to answer deep existential questions. I stopped overanalyzing and started to trust my instincts. I can just act and react because I have identified my triggers and have improved my conditioning.

But it's far from the end, as indicated by my recent outburst that got me canned at work.

What I've Learned

Two days after my hospitalization, at my therapist's insistence, I immediately wrote two vivid records: one describing that time, and the other covering the events that led up to it. It was important for me to understand how I got to a place where I was completely out of my comfort zone. I needed to find out why so that I could learn from it and not end up back on a gurney, drugged up, putting my family in hysterics and my life in someone else's hands.

I forced myself to learn that anyone with an ailment or shortcoming – including me, for sure – needs to adapt or die. Maybe I don't need to be so dramatic, but let's just agree that it's necessary for people like me to find adequate coping skills.

This is why I spend so much time learning about my disorder. I never want to feel helpless, struggling to manage my mood swings, making the same mistakes over and over while blaming other people.

The reason we struggle and suffer is because *we* have issues – not because of other people – and they can be addressed!

During my stay in the hospital, I accepted why I was there and had one of the greatest experiences in my life, bonding with a schizophrenic, someone with dissociative identity disorder, and homeless people I would have crossed the street to avoid.

The experience allowed me to appreciate the importance of recognizing and managing triggers and finding strategies to get back to a less emotional state. On top of that, or because of it actually, I learned to appreciate what I have in life.

The groups made me appreciate the power of peer support.

The groups cut down my learning curve.

When I'm doing well, I can offer a slice of my own experience to support other people on their journey.

I would love to provide a forum, a safe and secure space that can help other people find their normal too.

four

MENTAL HEALTH THROUGH PEER SUPPORT

Through college, I did not become as well-rounded, knowledgeable, and open-minded as my parents had intended. Instead, I became more insecure and pissed off.

But business school drilled into my head the importance of *best practices*, which describe techniques that are accepted as superior to any other and become the standard way of doing things. Think of best practices as the opposite of everything I was doing with my life.

I mention best practices because it applies to more than finding success in business. We can apply them to how we manage our mental health challenges – something that is not taught to us in school.

What has been my biggest challenge?

I've always felt like an outsider. I believe I am unrelatable to many people and want to be understood. There are few of us middle-class black Jews who attend Ivy League schools, or anywhere for that matter, who are forced to see the world from the outside looking in, or the position of the *other*.

Diversity aside, I'm on a journey, likely rockier than most, trying to achieve and maintain a healthier balance. I realize I can't do this on my own. I have had (and still need) unconditional support from my family who empower me and allow me to fail along the way.

Often, only those who unconditionally support us will forgive us when we sputter. Gym acquaintances and girlfriends are not as sympathetic. They may be more fun, but less forgiving.

Peer Influence and Support

I refer to AA as a model organization because it is a truly forgiving forum for *anyone* seeking redemption, maintenance, and self-improvement. These are also potential benefits of peer groups.

I believe the best approach to combat mood disorders is to find and maintain genuine support among our peers.

In peer groups, I touch upon a deep reserve of other people's lived experience. I actively listen to what others have done and are working on. I take these new concepts and ideas and review them with my treatment team of psychotherapists, behavioral therapists, and psychiatrist. I learn a little bit more about what I'm working on each week, and discuss what I learn with my group. This creates an effective snowball effect.

When I was at a total loss, not knowing where to turn, my father reached out to mental health support groups in

New York and stumbled upon a website that hadn't been updated in years but seemed to be worth a shot. We thought we had tried everything else by then, so why not?

Before I attended group, I struggled to take meds regularly. I was therapy-resistant and despised doctors for poisoning me with side effects while charging me a fortune. This changed when I attended a bipolar support group with two other members who openly discussed their medication.

From their exchange, I realized that my meds, specifically my antidepressant, could be contributing to my hypomania. A mood stabilizer might be a better alternative.

The next week I had my most productive discussion with my psychiatrist. I walked him through what I heard. We finally saw eye-to-eye. All because of a five-minute exchange in which I listened intently, and didn't say one word.

My cocktail of meds isn't a cure, but they stabilize my moods and allow me to develop my toolkit.

In another group session, someone mentioned behavioral therapy as an alternative to psychodynamic therapy.

A light bulb went on. *Eureka!*

I considered, on some level, that talk therapy was causing me to *relive* my past traumas rather than work through them.

I had uncovered the underlying issues from my subconscious but couldn't work through them.

This is what group sessions are about. We share ideas among people with common problems who empathize. We learn new ways to approach our issues that can change our lives by giving us hope. We root for each other. No abstractions. No theories. Instead, we hear real-life stories from people who are learning and teaching, making us soldiers fighting the same wars. We learn how to involve other people – friends, family, and co-workers – in support roles.

When members come to meetings with stories of how group has changed their lives, we *kvell,* the Yiddish word for feeling delighted and proud to the point of tears for someone else's achievement.

Group definitely beats throwing our hands in the air and telling ourselves that we've done everything we could when in fact we haven't scratched the surface because we didn't even know where to dig.

Since I'm not an expert and can only speak from my personal experiences, I'll use *most* when I refer to those people who preach a cure for mental health but are likely selling snake oil. Therapies, medications, and groups are not there to *cure* us – their purpose is to make our lives a little better.

It is safe to say there is no benchmark for mental health development as there is in 12-step programs.

Could there be one, perhaps?

New members in AA who struggle in the pre-contemplation and contemplation phases might look to other members who are sober and tell themselves that they want to be in their shoes.

I want to be sober too!

The objective is clear. There is nothing abstract about action and maintenance in the stages of recovery.

A Pyramid of Peace Through Personal Development

Allow me to go out on a limb to offer my benchmark – one that is tangible and visible – for mental health growth.

In case you don't buy into what I write in the rest of this chapter, consider it one more thing you've tried and considered.

Abraham Maslow was a psychologist who believed people have a "pyramid of needs." His idea was that people don't care about fancy things until they've taken care of their basic needs. Nothing else is important until we're no longer hungry or thirsty. We don't think about a new car if we haven't eaten in three days. We don't worry if people like our sneakers if we don't own a coat and it's 10 degrees outside.

Maslow's work has helped me keep into perspective my needs, shortcomings, ambitions, insecurities, and lifelong purpose to be happy with who I am – flaws and all.

After our physical needs – water, food, and basic health – are met, we focus on security, like finding a place to live. Then we focus on social needs, such as forming a group of friends.

Once we are well-fed, safely ensconced in a place to live, and have people who love us and recognize us for good things we've done, we can become concerned with bigger things, like being world-famous.

Finally, when we're fully evolved, we get to a point where we do not need fame and focus on strengthening our purpose in life.

MICHAEL J. HOFFMAN

Maslow's Hierarchy of Needs

This is a theory in psychology proposed by Abraham Maslow in his 1943 paper "A Theory of Human Motivation," which was published in *Psychological Review*. Maslow subsequently extended the idea to include his observations of humans' innate curiosity.

His theories parallel many other theories of human developmental psychology, some of which focus on describing stages of growth in humans. He then decided to create a classification system that reflected the universal needs of society as its base and then proceeding to more acquired emotions.

Maslow's hierarchy of needs is used to study how humans partake in behavioral motivation. Maslow used the terms "physiological," "safety," "belonging and love," "social needs" or "esteem," and "self-actualization" to describe the pattern through which human motivations move. This means that in order for motivation to occur at the next level, each level must be satisfied within the individual themselves.

This fundamental theory is a key foundation to our understanding of how drive and motivation correlate when discussing human behavior.

Each of these individual levels contain a certain amount of internal sensation that must be met in order for an individual to complete their hierarchy. The goal is to attain the fifth level or stage: Self-actualization.

Source: Wikipedia

When I venture out of my comfort zone, I yearn for safety and security. I build relationships and find constructive ways to improve my environment. This pyramid helps me recognize my own *mishugas* (Yiddish for craziness).

Some people criticize Maslow's pyramid.

"What about homeless people who want to become star athletes?"

Maslow would say they are going to have a tough time making it to the NBA if they're hungry and thirsty, friendless, and without anyone there to look out for them.

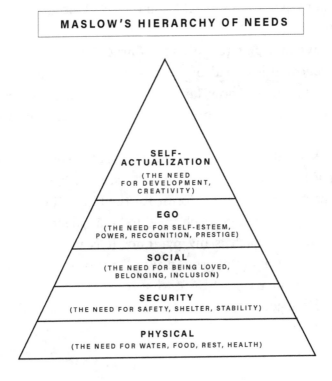

MASLOW'S HIERARCHY OF NEEDS

SELF-ACTUALIZATION
(THE NEED FOR DEVELOPMENT, CREATIVITY)

EGO
(THE NEED FOR SELF-ESTEEM, POWER, RECOGNITION, PRESTIGE)

SOCIAL
(THE NEED FOR BEING LOVED, BELONGING, INCLUSION)

SECURITY
(THE NEED FOR SAFETY, SHELTER, STABILITY)

PHYSICAL
(THE NEED FOR WATER, FOOD, REST, HEALTH)

We may be asking, what does Maslow's pyramid have to do with mental health?

Good question!

I believe it is better to visualize our mental health development in a pyramid hierarchy than discussed abstractly.

For years, I didn't know how to control my issues. I didn't have a large comfort zone. Once I left my apartment, most of what I tried to do was a struggle. I had very limited perspective outside of my negativity and pain. I had to accept that getting *weller* is a lifelong journey for which there are no shortcuts, and it's fine if I don't have all the answers right now.

When I faltered on my journey to *enlightenment*, my yellow brick road of *betterment*, I could have used a barometer to see how far I've come, not hate myself for where I *should* have been, give up, and then find myself having to start over.

Instead of hoping my mental health would improve, that I'd eventually find hope and "see the light," or gain perspective and see the "forest for the trees," I constructed a more hands-on approach to address my mental health.

My approach is my pyramid. It is my visual aid to remind me I'm *not* at ground zero. I am progressing. It sets me on a course to recognize what to work on next.

Here you can see my mental health pyramid. I'll walk you up it:

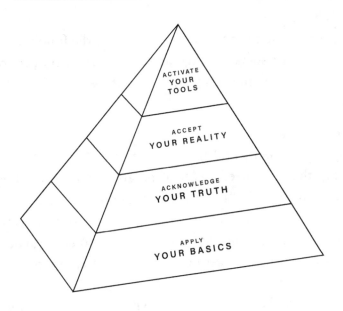

MY PERSONAL MENTAL HEALTH PYRAMID

ACTIVATE
YOUR
TOOLS

ACCEPT
YOUR REALITY

ACKNOWLEDGE
YOUR TRUTH

APPLY
YOUR BASICS

Align Your Layers

The pyramid represents our personal mental health journey. The layers offer a way to see our progression from one phase to another. Each layer illustrates a general baseline for us to see where we currently are, where we would like to be, and what we need to do to get there.

Apply Your Basics

Maintaining daily fundamentals is crucial and offers us a good barometer for measuring our progress. It begins when our alarm goes off in the morning: Get up on time, take a shower, brush our teeth, shave whatever needs shaving, make and drink coffee, wear appropriate clothing, lock and leave our apartment, and get to wherever we need to be – hopefully to our job.

But that's not all.

Our fundamentals may also include the following: See a therapist or social worker, attend an outpatient program, go to a group meeting, and do our best to form basic relationships.

Acknowledge Your Truth

Anyone whose mental health issues put them at risk must realize that they need to see a therapist and explore taking meds. Claims like, "I just want to find my magic pill" or "I just want to be happy" are common and understandable at this level, but they need to accept there is no perfect cocktail and we take meds to get incrementally better, not to cure all our problems.

People here can hold down a job or a volunteer opportunity but struggle at times working with co-workers and maintaining a regular schedule.

If our recurring issues never get resolved, acknowledging that truth is a key to work through them.

Accept Your Reality

We all need to build a strong network of support. This begins by recognizing that certain things we do and certain people we associate with might not be good for our mental health. We need to learn what triggers us and the extent they impact our well-being.

In behavioral therapy, we recognize these triggers and apply techniques to keep them in check.

We also need to accept that bipolar is no excuse for being a jerk.

How many of us can look back on our job history and say something like, "If I had been in my employer's shoes, I would have fired me, too?" Viewing experiences through this lens means we are taking responsibility for our own mess-ups, and that's good! It's a sign of growth. We have accepted the reality we need to make a change. The world doesn't need to change – and likely never will change – to accommodate us.

Activate Your Tools
Knowing our triggers and knowing what to do when they manipulate us into an uncomfortable or dangerous emotional state, represents a huge step forward. It means we have identified the catalysts for our mood shifts.

We can devise strategies to combat our mental health challenges rather than default to our lesser subconscious instincts. We can employ our tools when we find ourselves slipping.

Everything we learn from here on out is not an epiphany to celebrate. It's just one more tool to add to our toolkit.

We have separated ourselves from our disorder. It no longer defines who we are.

Putting Levels into Context
Many people with mood disorders reach a milestone and then stop their routine. From my experience seeing so many people in various peer groups, this is a common theme, and

carries big risks. These people rarely get better on their own. They white-knuckle their way through their next roadblock, and then find themselves battling yet another manic or depressive episode that lands them back to square one.

The pyramid helps to remind us that we need to stay on our *Meds* when we're well, not just when we're struggling.

Self-improvement is a lifelong process.

Here's another common theme I've heard repeatedly:

"I've tried everything so I'm attending a meeting or seeing a new therapist as a last resort."

Accepting that you need to see a specialist is usually one of the first steps – not the last resort – but it's a huge step to acknowledge your truth. Seeing a therapist isn't a cure, it's a highly recommended and proven avenue to help us find new tools to improve.

Another Dreadful but Far Too Common Scenario

I often meet with peers who find an effective medication regimen but then experience an undesirable side effect. Maybe we gain a few extra pounds or experience a light tremor. Since some of us have not accepted our reality, that side effect is all we see after being well for a while. We lose sight of the medication's efficacy.

Some people say, "I'm fine, why would I continue to put up with these side effects? It's not worth it."

Rather than consult with a doctor or check in with a peer, we stop taking medication, fall back into the same spiral that mandated taking meds in the first place, and experience yet another debilitating episode, leading to another hospitalization.

That's the difference between acknowledging your truth and accepting your reality.

Truth be told, the *light* is everywhere. It's above us and beneath us. In fact, we're in it right now, because when we maintain this perspective and put in the work, we always know where we are, regardless of any upward or downward swings.

Our hard-earned, uphill ascent actually gets easier and easier as our foundation grows stronger and stronger. At each level, the air becomes lighter as we accept more of what we need to add and accept what we need to remove. Our lives become more manageable and rewarding.

Why Some People Ascend More Rapidly Than Others

After thousands of hours in peer support groups, I've come to notice why some members improve their mental health more rapidly than others:

1. They are willing to commit to getting better, first by showing up, on time, on a regular basis. Woody Allen said that 90 percent of life is showing up. That applies here, too. No one forces us to attend. It is our choice.

2. They have positive body language. Instead of slouching indifferently they lean in to listen, even when the topic doesn't concern them.

3. They function well in group settings and avoid taking constant breaks, like to the restroom or to get water. Instead, they sit through an entire meeting

so that they don't miss hearing something useful and to offer their support.

4. They don't ask questions just to make themselves appear smarter or to become the center of attention. They listen to those who offer a different perspective.

5. They come to group with specific topics which they've been working on with their team of therapists, psychiatrists, friends, or from what they've been reading, and then they ask the group to help them find a solution.

For example, "I have an issue taking this medication because it hasn't helped as much as I'd like with anxiety, and I have trouble sleeping, too. So, what do you guys take for how I described my mood disorder?"

This is more constructive than something like, "I tried meds, but they don't work for me, so I want to try something new, so tell me what works, okay?"

6. They realize that life's problems won't go away just because we get more sleep, take new meds, get a girlfriend or find a better job. The ascent is about making life a little better for ourselves – not finding a cure.

I equate it to training for a marathon. The first step is to buy running shoes and commit. We carve out time to run, follow a routine, eat healthily, work with a trainer or a group to stay motivated, and slowly, week by week, we improve. We don't roll out of bed the day of the race and expect to run a personal best. Therapy is no different.

7. They focus on others, which may seem counter-intuitive, but it's not. Thinking of others is an effective practice of mindfulness; we get outside our own minds and accept the sharing of others. I believe this humility and generosity of spirit comes back to these people in good ways.

The Story of Carolyn

Carolyn is what support groups are all about. At the time we met, she was just shy of 50 years old, wasn't working, struggled to manage her depression and anxiety, and in her words, "I felt like I had done irreparable damage to my life."

Carolyn had attended group for years. When she started in mine, Carolyn reported that she got winded walking her dog down the block.

She committed to change. She listened to other members and knew change was possible.

Carolyn attended faithfully every Wednesday and Friday. She asked to volunteer before and after each group. She put up signs in a six-story pre-war building with limited ventilation, and then signed people in with a warm smile on her face, welcoming everyone with, "You made it; I'm so glad you're here!"

The one block soon progressed to two blocks which took her to Central Park.

Her new goal was to walk the 6.2-mile loop.

After a few months Carolyn walked the full loop every day – in rain, snow, or extreme heat and humidity. After a few more she progressed to two loops a day.

With spiritual and financial support from several dozen members, Carolyn walked the entire New York City Marathon in 2016.

She wore her completion medal proudly at the next meeting. Everyone waited to congratulate her because they felt that they had also accomplished a monumental feat.

We were just as excited when Carolyn did it again in 2017.

This is a clear and beautiful example of how focusing on other people's well-being can improve our own mental health. Carolyn showed that to all of us.

How Will We Ascend the Pyramid?

Our ability to ascend is not time-boxed. Some people progress significantly in a few months after a major episode. For others, this process can take years. Some people are content and able to maintain by seeing a therapist or attending a group every once in a while. Others have greater needs or ambitions and put in more time and effort to prioritize their mental health.

The mental health pyramid must be customized for each of us; it is constantly changing and needs revisiting from time to time. It takes time and effort to learn about what works better for us and how we can better manage our triggers. Using the knowledge that we pick up along the way, we gradually add more tools and a deeper understanding of our conditioning. This allows us to continue to ascend, but only when we are mentally equipped and motivated to take the next steps.

When our environment enables us, it can become too comfortable and inconvenient to change. It could be a parent who lets us loaf around without paying rent, or the government paying more assistance than a full-time job. I don't want to go through the psychology behind how some personality traits deal with adversity better than others, but rather point out that our comfort zone has to be a little uncomfortable. We will not change our habits if there is no catalyst for change.

Defining Our Own Mental Health Group

When we accept that we need to work with a therapist and participate regularly in a support group – potentially for the rest of our lives – our learning curve increases significantly. We are committed to a life of wellness.

And even if we find the world's greatest therapist, the Robin Williams character in *Good Will Hunting* – blessed with patience, insight, and an Academy Award – we must continue to put in the work in between sessions.

A good therapist can be good ONLY if they have a good patient.

The same principle applies to peer groups. We need to put ourselves in a room with other people who have either reached a place where we would like to be or are on par with us and have a similar goal to ascend.

How is someone who is struggling to get out of bed, eating their next meal and finding safety and security, going to relate to a high-powered attorney who is having a hard time limiting her hours so she can spend more time with her husband and children? Both of them can see the same therapist in separate appointments, but they cannot co-exist in the same peer group.

In many ways, our mental health can improve only as much as our environment allows. I will always feel for someone who is just coming to terms with their mood disorder, but to be honest, I won't learn anything from them.

In a meeting with people struggling with basic day-to-day functioning, like the desperados I encountered in the hospital, I can feel good helping them improve their situation, but it won't provide me with any real opportunity to grow. I like to bond and be validated for my progression, but when there is no growth potential it is not terribly satisfying.

This is why it's so important to find a complementary group and not just throw everyone together in one room, disregarding their level, and hoping the group runs itself.

We also cannot turn away people who do not seem to meet our high standard.

This is a challenge I am trying to address.

In the next two chapters, I will explore the challenges that these mixed groups present, including what peer group facilitators must learn to navigate and my ideas for a new concept in peer group design.

five

UNIVERSAL SUPPORT

New parents don't come home from the hospital thinking that their baby will be diagnosed years later with a mood disorder. Along with their hospital bill, they don't receive a complimentary guidebook on how to support a loved one who might develop mental health issues.

So, when their kids begin acting weird, I'm guessing most parents don't know what to do.

Most of the time parents manage the basics quite well. They feed us, bathe us, clothe us, teach us, and love us pretty damn well. The more *invested* ones read books from Oprah's *Live From the Library*, or whatever is the latest and greatest source of truth, and praise their kid's accomplishments to just about anyone who will listen.

And when most parents receive negative feedback from outsiders, like from another parent or teacher, it creates a cognitive discord.

How can my kid be bad? That would make me a bad parent, wouldn't it?

My mother and father saw me go nuts. But they weren't therapists. They gave me a stable, loving home, while telling me at times I belonged in a stable!

What started as fussing during my childhood soon became World War III. They had little tolerance and no remedies.

Maybe John Lennon was wrong; with some kids you need more than love.

Didn't my parents understand? Couldn't they hear what was going on in my head?

I CAN'T HELP IT!

I DON'T KNOW WHY!

WHAT'S WRONG WITH ME?

They called me an ingrate, a spoiled brat – along with more colorful names – which only made me feel worse. I hated myself because I couldn't get better, and resented people for not caring enough to help.

I don't blame teachers and bosses for disregarding my needs. God bless the few who really tried. But it really hurts to know that some parents throw their hands in the air as if to say, "I'm trying!" and do little else.

I know my parents have done and always will do the best they can to support me. I wasn't the easiest kid in the neighborhood to raise. It might be easier to raise a rebel who stays out late, experiments and deceives you (cough, cough, my older brother), which we attribute to adolescence or going through a phase, than be forced to support someone for several years who is an angel one minute, and a f-ing lunatic the next.

So, here's my point: Love is not enough. Neither is sympathy, patience, and good intentions.

Okay, then. Got it. As a supporter, what do I do?

Family Advocates

I once attended a support group where someone praised *Bipolar Survival Guide*, by David J. Miklowitz. He described it as, "Everything you wanted to know about the *illness* but were afraid to ask." As a Woody Allen fan, I appreciated the reference.

He told us it explained the disorder's causes, diagnosis, and treatments, and anyone could embrace it, not just someone struggling with mental health.

This is *precisely* why groups are so important. I never would have heard of the book if I hadn't attended that session!

As soon as I finished the book, I begged my parents to read it. I knew it would provide a much-needed fresh perspective since my incessant "why don't you fucking get me?" had grown tiresome and didn't convey what I really needed.

After reading the book, my dad told me, "I felt like I was re-experiencing your entire life through other people's true-to-life stories."

It took time for my parents to understand what bipolar disorder is, but when they did, they became my strongest advocates. That was a hell of a lot better than being my biggest disappointment.

They attended support groups, read everything worth reading, and after getting my permission (I gave it gladly!)

openly discussed my disorder with other people they knew who had children of their own with mental health challenges. They even drove in from Philadelphia for a same-day appointment at the Bipolar Family Center in New York City.

Back at work, when I was ostracized by my project team, when I was put on probation, and when I was convinced the world was conspiring against me, my father emailed Dr. Miklowitz. Miklowitz referred my father to a renowned psychiatrist at the University of Pennsylvania – my alma mater. The doctor agreed to meet with me before my Monday morning commute to the client site. That doctor, in turn, changed my meds to curb my aggression and obsessive thinking. With her help I got through the rest of the assignment less scathed.

So, here's the moral of that story: We're more likely to get better when we have committed people around us who support and enable our growth, rather than dismiss our concerns and blame us for our shortcomings. My parents, at last, accepted the reality that most of my issues in life stemmed from a poorly managed and misunderstood mood disorder.

Yes, I am fortunate!

Too many people have parents, friends, and even lovers who believe that mood disorders are a crutch and a sign of weakness.

And though I appreciate the support, it doesn't extend much further than my parents' willingness to help. Most co-workers don't give me slack when I have a bad day. Few *friends* support my group (*NO*, "short bus" is not a catchy name!). And my parents' suggestions (i.e. well-intended advice) is kerosene on an off day.

As hard as it's been, I've had to accept that I, Michael Hoffman, am solely responsible for building a network of supportive people and must learn to cope when they can't be there for me.

What does that look like?

They are a group of people who *get it*. They are people who understand that I'm unwell at times, not ill all the time.

What happens when I find them?

- I make sure they don't enable me.

- I reciprocate so we don't form a one-sided co-dependent relationship.

- I educate them so they know when and how to support me, which is only necessary some of the time, not a 24/7 life sentence.

- I need not get discouraged, or discourage them, if I feel like they are not doing enough.

- I accept that these people will not always be around.

What's the end goal?

Over time, we add tools to get stronger mentally. We rely less on other people's goodwill, become more self-sufficient, and pay it forward.

This is the apex of My Personal Mental Health Pyramid – loosely inspired by *The 36th Chamber of Shaolin*!

Universal Support Pyramid

When we assess our ability to support other people, I point to the Universal Support Pyramid.

The Pyramid shows where we are helping and where we can help even more.

Since this is ultimately a book about my interest in expanding peer group outreach, I created the support pyramid in the context of advocacy roles in peer groups. But since the pyramid must extend beyond the four walls of a support group, I created a universal pyramid, for any advocate in any context.

Each layer represents a particular level of an advocate's function:

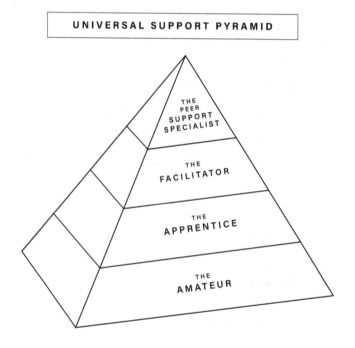

UNIVERSAL SUPPORT PYRAMID

THE PEER SUPPORT SPECIALIST

THE FACILITATOR

THE APPRENTICE

THE AMATEUR

The Amateur

I believe everyone in our network has the right intentions – to help us when we're not in a good place – but it's important to recognize how capable someone is to provide the support we need.

It's because of the support amateurs provide that we hear the clichéd expression, "You can choose your friends, not your family," and validates the need for peer support.

Amateurs passively listen to us as a courtesy but they typically do not empathize with our plight. I think the best description for them is *sounding board.*

When they grow impatient, they give us advice without fully understanding our point of view. When we don't take their advice, they often dismiss us with, "Well, if you're not going to take my advice then you're on your own," as in, if it works for them then it must work for everyone.

We try to give them credit for taking the time but we often feel worse after the exchange. Their misguided advice usually causes a rift in the relationship since both parties grow frustrated.

Thanks for nothing!

When we tell them why their advice hasn't worked and what we've tried instead – like medication – they'll ask us, "Why would you take that?"

People in our circle who do not rise past Amateur can be too triggering. They either need to be trained or possibly cut out of our lives.

The Apprentice

I put my father and most supportive people who try to understand mood disorders but don't completely empathize in this tier.

Apprentices take time and effort to learn. They read and watch TV shows capturing mental health challenges, like Op-Eds from different publications, and *Homeland*, which for the most part accurately depicts what it's like to live with bipolar. They tend to give theoretical or second-hand advice because it's hard for them to share from their own lived experience.

Apprentices provide a much lighter touch than amateurs because they understand there is a gray area with what works and doesn't work, rather than what people should and shouldn't do, and give us credit for trying new things and working through adversity.

Most build an effective toolkit for offering support but get thrown off when their input works one day and gets a nasty response the next.

We really should come with instructions!

Fortunately, they do not get discouraged easily and keep us accountable. We appreciate that they make the effort.

The Facilitator

I won't get too much into the facilitator's role in a group just yet. I will provide the characteristics for what makes this person capable to run one later on.

Facilitators empathize. Most have a mood disorder that they acknowledge and accept. They are not therapists but they know which anecdotes to share from their lived experience that will resonate with others.

Facilitators have a full toolkit that they offer such as psychodynamic therapy, behavioral therapy, medications, meditative practices, and other healthy outlets.

Facilitators make great peers because they recognize when other people are declining and put in time and effort to help.

I currently put myself in this category.

The Peer Support Specialist

Peer support specialists are fully trained in crisis management. They have an action plan for every scenario. Most have seen and heard everything.

When peer support specialists don't speak, they actively listen. In other words, they offer nonverbal cues to show understanding (nodding, eye contact, leaning forward) while building trust and rapport.

Specialists extrapolate from their own lived experience to any subject. They can engage with someone with bipolar just as easily as they can with someone recently diagnosed with breast cancer or someone struggling with spousal abuse.

Not all are professionals, but many make careers as social workers and therapists.

Watching a good peer support specialist in action is inspiring.

How do Advocates Ascend?

I believe empathy is the foundation for peer support.

Empathy comes easier for someone with a mood disorder because it forces them to battle, learn from the experience, and find new coping strategies to thrive. However, advocates do not need to have a mood disorder or know someone with a mood disorder to empathize.

Empathy can be acquired and grow organically.

Some people who are close-minded and believe mood disorders are a crutch, an "excuse to do nothing productive in life," to "sponge off federal government for assistance," or even claim "psychiatry is a racket for the Jews" (true story!), likely won't ascend the peer support pyramid any time soon.

The first step to rise from Amateur to Apprentice is to accept that mental health issues exist and need to be managed with a light touch. When we acknowledge a friend or family member has a mood disorder, we make a choice. We either continue with the aforementioned amateur nonsense, like probe and give advice, or take proactive steps to offer real support.

The progression is often gradual. When advocates attend support groups or therapy sessions for several months or a few years, they pick up a few insights. If no groups are available, they learn by reading books to help build their foundation to acquire new support tools.

As for rising from Apprentice to Facilitator and to Peer Support Specialist, I know several members from family support groups who become excellent facilitators and acquire skills necessary to specialize.

Ascension takes effort. It's a commitment.

As a crash course, here's what I've learned over the years facilitating several hundreds of groups....

When Should a Facilitator Jump in?

To a new member, group can be overwhelming. It can also be a lot to handle for a new facilitator. As a facilitator, it's our responsibility to take control of the space, but not in a heavy-handed way.

Here are some situations that may require our intervention:

1. *When people are being disruptive and not obeying the rules.*

    Sometimes it's easy to restore order if someone checks their phone during group. Just remind them that other people are sharing when they are on their phone, and that if it's urgent they should step outside or otherwise turn it off and put it away.

    We don't have to say a word. A quick smile and nod usually do the trick and doesn't disrupt the rest of the group or make the person feel bad if it is an urgent call or text. If issues persist, I'll give them a warning. I'll issue a second warning if necessary, and take them outside to reaffirm the guidelines, where I can tell them this group meeting might not be the best fit for them right now. If I have to, I'll walk them over to see the coordinator or bring them to the exit, all the while emphasizing the group policy.

2. *When people use blanket statements instead of personal statements.*

For example, "I read in the paper that . . ." or "Someone mentioned to take this medication . . ." are not a good idea. To personalize a statement, I try asking it another way, such as, "Is that something you tried or would consider?" and if they answer no, I'll ask the entire group something like, "Has anyone else tried that or something similar?"

3. *When a topic is not relevant.*

In the midst of a moment like this, I'm inclined to say something like, "We came here to discuss our moods, so let's shelve that specific topic until after group." From there I trust the group to be my eyes and ears.

This came up in one of the first meetings I attended, in which someone brought up *Silver Linings Playbook* when discussing how bipolar is portrayed in the mainstream media. We ended up hijacking the entire meeting talking about Jennifer Lawrence's Academy Award and her work in *Hunger Games*. None of this directly related to mood disorders, but the facilitator let it go on. The discussion lifted our spirits and built camaraderie.

For the most part that's fine, as long as we don't let it take over the meeting or isolate someone who has come in to address something more pressing.

It's a judgment call.

4. *When we notice other members are uncomfortable with a particular discussion.*

When we see other people uncomfortable or uninterested in a topic (arms crossed, yawning, looking at watch, playing with hair) then it's time for the facilitator to intervene. I often trust the group to be my eyes and ears. They signal when they want me to jump in.

5. *When some members are less communicative.*

In my group introduction I remind everyone that they're not obligated to share. I touch base with the group with roughly 15 minutes left to invite less talkative members by alluding to their intro and connecting it to what we discussed. Even if they still don't want to share, they'll appreciate that I made the effort.

Once I made this small gesture and wound up speaking to a member after group for two hours.

6. *When people speak too much.*

If someone becomes grandiose or manic or simply hogs the spotlight, I try to find one specific thing that they shared that I believe will resonate with the rest of the group. Once I validate them for it, I can open up that topic to the whole group or to specific members who haven't spoken, to draw them into the discussion.

For example, if someone goes on and on about how much work sucks and how they want to kill their co-workers – something I can definitely relate to but try not to entertain – I'll gently cut them off and say something like:

"I think it's great that you brought up triggers at work, and I believe Brian, James, and Debbie raised something similar in their introduction. Is there anything you guys want to add?"

The group will appreciate that I intervened and opened the discussion to everyone else. Also, by not asking a direct question to one person but rather to a few people, I don't put anyone on the spot.

How to Give Advice

No matter how well-intentioned and empathic we try to be, giving advice can be detrimental because it assumes the recipient has not yet tried what we suggest.

These assumptions are often made based on what we *think* we know about someone's life.

Consider these two approaches:

Scenario 1:

Jamie: "I try to manage my stress by exercising, but I have trouble getting started."

Maria: "You want to manage stress? You should wake up early to work out."

Jamie: "I would, but my meds won't let me get up in time."

Take note that this is a defensive response – understandably – which doesn't lead to a constructive discussion. But since a precedent has been set to allow direct advice, other people continue down that path:

> *Malik*: "Why don't you go after work instead, or find time on the weekends?"

> *Suzanne*: "You should talk to your doctor about switching your meds."

Instead, consider the following approach:

Scenario 2:

Jamie: "I try to manage my stress by exercising, but I have trouble getting started."

Maria: "Okay, I hear you. I try to exercise in the morning before work since I usually don't have time in the evening. It's tough, but I leave my workout clothes next to my alarm on the other side of the apartment."

Jamie: "I tried that, but my medication forces me to get at least eight hours of sleep, and besides a little grogginess I feel each morning they seem to work for me."

Malik: "I have that same problem, so I take advantage of my weekends to work out and go for long walks during the day."

Suzanne: "I do something similar, which really helps."

Jamie: "Yeah, interesting, that's something I could try. Thanks."

Speaking from the "I" perspective means not giving direct advice, which often leads to more fruitful dialogue. In the second scenario, no judgment has been passed on Jamie's medication or her habits. If Jamie wants to delve more deeply into her meds, then she can do so on her own terms.

It's natural to get defensive when other people try to fix our issues – especially strangers, and especially when we don't ask for it.

Their advice may come with good intentions, but it also comes with bias – how we look, how we present ourselves, and the little we've shared with them.

When we offer advice, it's as if we are telling them that we know how they should live their life better than they do. This rarely goes over well, especially when the person we speak to never asked for our help. When the person offering advice does not get the grateful reaction they expect or feel they deserve, it often sets up an inappropriate and defensive response, like:

"You don't listen to reason. Clearly this explains why you are where you are!"

Asking direct questions can prompt the same defensive reaction as offering unsolicited advice. Often the person asking the question is implying that they can quickly solve the problem and could imply that the recipient hasn't considered the question before.

Questions off the top of our head aimed at someone with mental health issues will most likely not create a miraculous, life-altering moment. It's just not realistic that hearing a few bullet points about someone's life can elicit a question so profound that it will be helpful. Plus, asking questions of someone we barely know is harmful because it puts that person on the spot to answer when they may not be ready.

People need to ask and answer these questions for themselves to learn and change their behaviors.

Facing Controversy

Suicide, on the other hand, is tricky. I routinely start meetings by asking, "Please let me know during your intro if you are in distress. If so, I will be happy to speak with you outside of group, so please don't hesitate to ask."

I once left the group after the intro to speak to a member one-on-one for an hour. I knew the more experienced members could manage the group and could grab me outside for escalations. Other times, I've taken members to the hospital – sometimes during, sometimes after group – while they process if they are at risk of self-harm.

More often though, we can address the most distressed members in group first and encourage everyone else to come to that person's aid. Even the more hypomanic members will appreciate adding some friendly reassurance.

How do I manage this?

I'll ask the group if it's okay to spend 10 to 15 minutes on them immediately after the intros.

What does this do?

The group will feel good helping, knowing it will not monopolize the entire discussion. Also, the member is not forced to sit through a full group uncomfortably and struggling, waiting until the last few minutes to talk.

Hearing from a distressed member late in group leads to an anti-climactic group experience. Ideally, we want to leave group upbeat.

Are You Ready for the Next Level?

While it's essential to know the basics of how to handle difficult topics, some topics require specific training techniques. Continuing education outside group helps strong facilitators become great peer support specialists.

Even the best facilitators and peer support specialists find it difficult to give equal time to someone completely depressed – without depressing the rest of the group – with someone hypomanic who will quickly dominate the discussion without making either feel isolated.

Maybe it's like a point guard in basketball trying to keep his long-distance shooters happy while also taking care of his big men under the basket!

California Dreamin'?

In March 2019 while on a brief hiatus from yet another bad situation at work, I attended a non-violent communication workshop in a notable hippie commune in Big Sur, California.

I carried out my ideal excursion from my 20s: Cruising in a new Ford Mustang convertible down the Pacific Coast Highway – San Francisco to Los Angeles with brief stops in Santa Cruz and San Luis Obispo – as a brief reprieve from the Big Apple.

Big Sur was the site of Don Draper's epiphany at the end of *Mad Men* where he envisions the world-famous Coke commercial.

Paradise!

I didn't even mind going from a comfy sound-proofed apartment in Manhattan to sleeping on a bunk bed above a 50-ish man with sleep apnea and chronic coughing fits.

The workshop was run by a disciple of Marshall Rosenberg, an American psychologist, mediator, author, and teacher who developed Nonviolent Communication in the early 1960s. The process supports partnership and resolving conflicts between people in personal relationships and within our general society.

During our second to last session, a senior exec from a major Fortune 100 company told us she was having issues communicating with her on-again, off-again boyfriend. Up until that moment, this woman had remained quite buttoned up, behaving in a much more corporate manner than the other 20 participants.

Apparently, her boyfriend was quite well-off but was noncommittal. She was looking for more constructive ways to tell him how much his actions hurt her so she could break the cycle.

Prior to that, she and I had shared some excellent discussions, including her telling me that if I lost my job, I could come work for her. I took this as an invitation to chime in with everyone else:

"Have you tried talking to him?"

"What does he say?"

"What makes you so attracted to him?"

"Can you confirm with him a day before?"

As she was being peppered with these questions, I geared up with one of my own:

"What makes him so enthusiastic a week before and so noncommittal the day before, or on the day of the supposed trip? Couldn't you try something else to keep him accountable?"

It was one question too many. As soon as I was done, she took a deep breath and turned to the instructor, obviously distraught.

"I feel like I'm being attacked," she said.

A few minutes later, I tried to apologize. She coldly responded that it was okay. When I asked to sit with her during lunch, she shook her head.

"Not now."

That was it. She didn't speak to anyone from our group again. We all meant well, and all wanted to help, but by giving direct, unsolicited advice we were assuming that she hadn't tried any of the many things we suggested.

If only we had shared what had worked for us and allowed her to process and contribute when she was ready, she might have received more useful tools and I might be taking weekly excursions to Hilton Head instead of regurgitating this interaction in a cramped shared office space in midtown Manhattan.

Being an effective and empathic facilitator is a work in progress.

We're always learning.

six

MY PEER GROUP DESIGN

I will always be on a journey to support mental health, for me and for others.

When people thank me for helping them, they're forgetting we're all in this together. Today I'm helping them; tomorrow they'll help me. That's the way group works.

It's rewarding when I can support people through their struggles, validate them for opening up, and share my insights to help them find new coping strategies.

In return, I learn from other people working on more complex issues to meet their longer-term goals, and reinforce my discipline talking to novices. The time I spend on others gives me less time to ruminate on my issues.

This is how I activate my tools.

When I left the hospital in 2013, I accepted my bipolar condition in a relatively short timeframe, and embraced my role as an advocate. I attended support group meetings every Wednesday and Friday. I allowed myself to cry profusely in one meeting with 15 people when I finally accepted that I had a mood disorder and would need to take meds for the rest of my life. My neighbor, a complete stranger, commended me for my strength.

One of the few times I could take a compliment to heart. I remember this so I can pay it forward.

The meds, and all my peer support meetings, have not and will not cure me, but they have made my life a whole lot more manageable.

When I got more stable, I could finally apply what I learned over years in therapy. I spent more time addressing specific issues head-on than trying to resolve more deep-seated psychological problems.

I don't wake up hoping I'll get through the day. I wake up feeling how I'm feeling, accept whatever state I'm in, and if I feel off, I employ one of my many tools before I start my day.

I created a wonderful cycle of listening, accepting, learning, and strategizing, all to help me become more tolerant, self-aware, tolerable, and effective.

Now I'm ready for the next level....

Embracing New Revelations

Once I stabilized, kept a full-time job for several months, and had a pretty good routine going, I became a fixture at the Mood Disorders Support Group (MDSG) in New York City where I ran the operations, managed both sites, coordinated and facilitated groups, and sat on the board.

Running mental health groups through an established non-profit is far easier than starting one from scratch.

And growing, maintaining, coordinating, and facilitating, etc....

Running a group from scratch that tries to limit its member base to working professionals that also tries to remove the stigma of mental health is an even bigger challenge.

Most working professionals cannot afford to be linked to mental illness in any way. Maybe someday – the same way people with other illnesses and conditions are – but as a society we are not there yet.

As I write this, a gay man is running for president. Ads are running on TV for betting on NBA games. Banks are lending to marijuana dealers. I'm confident that mood disorders will be just another socially-accepted and politically-disputed issue.

Similar to where we once were with gay marriage, legalized gambling, and weed, it's hard to imagine that mood disorders will ever be mainstreamed until the day they are. Until then, I'll gladly work with people who are willing to advocate for reform, though I believe my time is better spent appealing to a more targeted group on the ground floor.

Openly gay politicians started small in uber liberal districts in the '70s with Elaine Noble in Massachusetts and Harvey Milk in San Francisco. Marijuana started to legalize on the state level – not federal – with Colorado and California. Gambling grew because it's a quick win revenue stream for politicians, but the same logic applies – it's still accepted.

My objective is not to mitigate stigma and preach acceptance on a global scale. Not even Harold Hill (*The Music Man*) could sell acceptance when many people process *undiagnosed-serial-killer-lunatic* bipolar illness more often than *slightly-erratic-but-contained* bipolar condition.

Whether we choose to attend a group and find new strategies to improve our mental health has nothing to do with wealth and social standing or a lack of it.

I would like to include the lower socio-economic crowd like those from the hospital. But the group I'm trying to create *might* not be the best fit for them.

I equate my approach to target more high-powered professionals to the executive poker game Tony ran in *The Sopranos*. High rollers don't play $2 to $4 limit poker. We need a forum for them, too.

We all have different things to lose in life when we rock our mental boats.

I want to create a targeted group because nothing like it presently exists. The group can fill a niche that these people currently do not explore because mental illness often comes with bias, is misunderstood in many circles, and can result in people losing their jobs and relationships.

Everyone can use a safe space to discuss their thoughts, emotions, and actions constructively with others.

Protecting Stigmas

Imagine how disastrous it would be for a lawyer if she shows up to group, gains a lot of insight from interacting with a financial trader and a screenwriter about stress management, but then one of her clients who is paying her $400/hr. finds out and puts pressure on the law firm to replace her, derailing her path to partnership. Whether her colleagues *should've* accepted the lawyer for finding better coping strategies is irrelevant. The financial trader, screenwriter, and those in countless other white-collar professions tend to be more forgiving.

If instead she attended AA meetings twice a week or saw a psychotherapist for the same issues, it would be more accepting. Some might commend her for taking proactive measures to manage stress. Even if she were taking benzodiazepines such as Xanax or Valium, no one would question her as long as she were meeting or exceeding expectations.

"Bipolar" sends a much different message.

Since I cannot change the stigma assigned to *mental illness*, I'll need to distance the association to lead a successful peer support organization.

Being an advocate means having to accept that there is a stigmatizing label.

What does all this lead to?

I cannot run a bipolar support group! I can only run a peer group where some of us just happen to share bipolar histories. We meet to find strategies to more effectively manage stress, anxiety, and lulls in mood because we work long hours, often get little sleep, and must use everything at our disposal to cope, maintain, and grow.

The messaging matters. Controlling the narrative is paramount.

My Peer Group Design

Everything I have shared from my mental health battles to how I perceive seasoned members and facilitators has led me to my design for a peer support group.

Here is a more detailed view:

Mission Statement

Foster a confidential and non-judgmental forum to discuss ideas proactively and strategies to improve our mental health and wellness. Run by seasoned facilitators with lived experience for members who are accepting of, and are actively working to improve, their mental health.

Objectives

1. Find camaraderie with other members who empathize and do not judge.

2. Discuss topics that the rest of the world does not appreciate or understand.

3. Learn from other members' lived experience.

4. Share insights from our own experience that resonate with other members.

5. Be held accountable in pursuit of long-term goals.

Guidelines

1. Group is confidential

   What happens in group stays in group.

2. Group is non-judgmental

Members share from the "I" perspective.

3. Group members do not give advice

   We make exceptions only if members ask for it.

4. Group members cannot ask direct questions

   We encourage members to share on their terms. Questions are permitted but need to be directed to the group.

Meeting of the Minds

Meeting of the Minds offers peer support groups to promote mental health and wellness and non-judgmental listening and learning.

The group encourages discussions that allow members to acknowledge their truths, accept their realities, and activate their tools.

Meeting of the Minds welcomes anyone who adheres to the guidelines, policies, and procedures.

Meetings are run by well-trained facilitators and peer support specialists who:

- Ensure groups remain healthy, safe, and respectful.

- Promote constructive discussions to generate ideas and strategies.

- Offer sufficient time for every member to contribute.

- Use discretion to intervene to run an optimal group.

Focus

Meeting of the Minds offers peer support groups to anyone

interested in finding effective strategies to better manage stress, anxiety, and other mild to moderate issues.

The groups address more current issues that impact mental health. The groups do not focus on deep-seated unresolved issues for which members are encouraged to address with psychodynamic therapists. The groups are not meant to be a substitute for therapy.

Frequent Topics Include

- Mitigate stigmas.

- Improve interpersonal relationships.

- Open the door to new therapies or treatments.

- Referrals to proven clinicians who can help to improve our mental health.

Group Schedule

7 to 7:30: Check-in with a volunteer

- Every member who RSVPs is given a name tag.

- Snacks and beverages (non-alcoholic) will be served.

- Cellphones and note taking are not allowed in group.

7:30 to 8:45: Peer Group

- Members take 30 seconds to 2 minutes to introduce themselves. Members raise what they are working on and what they are looking to get from the group.

- Volunteer closes group at 7:45 to protect the safety and containment of the group in progress.

- Majority of the group is spent cross-talking.

- Facilitator checks in around 8:30 to cover any topics that have not been addressed and to hear from less active members.

- Facilitator starts to close group around 8:40.

8:45 to 9:00: Follow up

- Facilitators and members share referrals to other mental health support avenues, e.g. therapists, similar groups, other wellness activities.

Target Consumer

How will we know what the ideal attendee looks like? How can we cater to that person?

- Working professional.

- Someone who understands that the goal is not to eradicate triggers – just to mitigate them. They will continue to engage in stressful activities and will find better ways to cope.

- Someone who sees a regular therapist and either actively takes medication to stabilize their mood, or at least keeps an open mind to medication.

- Someone no longer searching for the *magic pill* and understands that working through mood-related issues is a journey, doesn't get discouraged easily, and might even enjoy the process.

- Someone who doesn't take shortcuts and explores all avenues to improve their mental health.

- Someone who acknowledges their truth and accepts their reality.

Who Is an Ideal Attendee in an Under 25 Group?

To keep members focused on relatable issues, it helps to separate groups by age range.

- A college student, graduate student, or young professional who is having issues adjusting to a daily regimen.

- Someone who accepts they drink too much or experiments with recreational drugs and wants to break these destructive patterns.

- Someone discouraged that their meds "don't or haven't been working for them" and who wants to know what would work better.

- Someone willing to spend money for support but would prefer a cost-effective therapist or psychiatrist, either in network or on a sliding scale.

- Someone with a supportive person in their life who does not fully understand what they're going through and could use a more constructive forum with people their age who empathize.

- Someone who applies most of their basics and is looking to fully acknowledge their truth.

Models to Follow

Why doesn't a global peer support group exist like AA and other 12-step programs?

There are several peer groups, but they are not as effective for professionals who make six figures and cannot afford to be branded with mental illness. They could use a less stigmatizing group.

I want to make this happen. I am asking the right questions, but I don't yet have all the answers. Like with my personal development and mental health journey, it will take a while to build the right model; but I believe I will succeed because enough people have a vested interest to see their own and other people's mental health improve.

Here are some things to consider for my peer group design:

Quality Control Standards
Perfect policies and procedures before growing the organization.

I think of Ray Kroc, the (supposed) founder of McDonald's, who applied the same model from the first restaurant in San Bernardino, CA to other locations, and employed ambitious, humble, hard-working individuals with a vested interest in seeing the business grow. This is similar to the committed, capable individuals who run chapters in AA.

Process
Replicate the AA model to run multiple groups in multiple locations.

AA welcomes participants from different socioeconomic backgrounds. At any meeting you may see a Fortune 500 executive sitting next to someone who just got out of prison or decided to take a brief hiatus from skid row.

This works because AA does not permit cross-talk between members. All communication runs directly through the moderator.

This raises an important question to anyone who facilitates: How can we ensure the members relate to each other, and how do we find capable facilitators who can manage the group if they don't?

Policies
Guidelines and policies need to be updated and accessible to facilitators and members.

Technology
Either continue to use Meetup, manage groups through a separate website, or both.

I've run several successful groups through Zoom during the coronavirus pandemic. This will continue to be a good alternative for those who do not have a group nearby.

Business Model
Either create a non-profit 501(c)(3), like MDSG, and apply for grants, build a for-profit business, or possibly both.

Oversight
For-profit requires a high touch to manage liabilities and field escalations. Non-profits like AA come with their own headaches but can prosper with less oversight.

Beyond Group

Meeting of the Minds' success hinges on perfecting one group before it can scale to other locations. The end goal is to operate in every city and every country in the world so that everyone has a safe and supportive forum to meet with their peers.

Until then, I will promote the values and best practices of peer support.

Being non-judgmental and supportive is not limited to four walls a few hours a week in remote locations.

seven

WHERE CAN I GO FROM HERE?

I'm not strapped down on a gurney right now, and don't expect to be on one ever again. I've assembled a toolkit to prevent anything like that from happening again, but I know it's still possible.

I'm bipolar, not insane.

It's lunacy to think history couldn't repeat itself. I will always look over my shoulder to make sure my past incidents don't become my present circumstance.

I have to commit to my daily routine.

Some days my toolkit feels rigid. Sometimes the rigidity feels worse than doing none of the things on my ever-growing list.

It's a balancing act. There's usually a middle ground.

My parents understand how fragile their son's state of mind is. They understand my potential; they know I can reach it if I keep working at it. If I don't get discouraged. If I take responsibility for my actions.

Sure, there are days when I'm slightly delusional; it goes with the territory. Can I really build a global peer support group? So what if I can't? Even if I fall way short of my grandiose plans, I can still build my current member base and find better ways to offer support. Every new member means I – WE! – are helping more people. That's a good enough reason to keep at it.

There is no shortage of people needing help.

I want to support others who may suffer like I sometimes do. You may be struggling, or someone you know and care about is struggling and needs help. You, or someone who could be you, have sat next to me in a group. I've listened to your stories. I've laughed with you. I've cried with you. I've gone home after countless support group meetings thinking of so many of you, not sad to hear that you've been saddled with poorly managed mood disorders, but happy to know that I am not the only one! We're not talking misery loves company; we're talking shared experiences. When one of us improves, the group as a whole improves. When one of us improves, it's another friendly reminder that our problems are manageable.

I hope that the stories in this book demonstrate the value of peer support groups.

The whole process starts with our commitment to take necessary steps.

Why I Believe in Group

Everyone has war stories about their bipolar history. Most of us think our story is unique. It can be isolating. Any time we may feel self-conscious, it's good to find out we are not alone.

Group is empathic.

We usually realize this two minutes into a support group. These are our peers. This is where we can be ourselves or that day's version of our self.

Group is non-judgmental.

When I started attending groups in 2012, I used to wait impatiently for other members to complete whatever it was they were sharing so I could speak. I was so anxious that I would say the wrong thing. Over time, I started to listen to what others have done or were trying to do. I looked for opportunities to connect their stories with other members' experiences to make it useful for everyone.

As a new facilitator, I was terrified I would say something triggering and entice some members to leave. In one of my first groups, a member got up 30 minutes before group ended while I struggled to connect two unrelated comments – one from someone depressed and one from someone hypomanic. I replayed the series of events for several weeks. I lost sleep. I wanted to give up.

What did I do wrong and what could I have done differently?

When the member returned, he apologized to me for leaving early. He forgot to mention in the intro that *he had to catch an earlier train!*

In that one exchange, my self-worth was restored from a stranger validating me.

Cognitive behavioral therapy refers to this as fortune telling – feeling as if the members all think that I'm a fugazi (fraud) – and catastrophizing – feeling that the one incident makes me unworthy to facilitate.

I realized two things that day: Stuff will happen. Some stuff could be on account of me. I cannot put too much importance on any single exchange and let it define me. I'm doing the best I can. Also, if my self-esteem is so fragile and I'm so easily triggered, I might need to reconsider facilitating and instead attend as a more passive member.

Our mental health comes first.

What Else I've Learned

To help stay grounded, I work on activities to be more present and to control triggers.

In key settings like work meetings, presentations, or even group, I over-prepare to mitigate stress and anxiety.

One of my bigger triggers is when I am told I did wrong or should do better, especially in public. I perceive it as extreme passive-aggression. Sometimes when I can't act on my impulse to lash out my whole body goes ice cold. I'd rather spend extra time to prep than feel inferior.

I can add work preparation to my toolkit.

Who I spend my time with also plays a major role in my mental health. Like most people, I'm cool when I'm with an ally who can help to keep me grounded. On the other hand, I'm not so good when I'm around people who I think are out to sabotage me, or *even* just ignore me. I try not to pass judgment and stay objective.

I also function better on airplanes, in movie theaters (one of my sanctuaries), in spin class, and anywhere people are talking and texting. I might even be okay again in a psych ward, but I prefer other options.

Some people may call me the n-word again, tell me or suggest to me in more subtle ways that I don't belong. That doesn't mean everyone thinks that way. Although when I'm at my worst I think most people do.

I can't change how people see the world and react to me trying to be the best version of me. I only have myself to blame when I resort to all-or-nothing or black-or-white thinking.

I've become more self-aware and trust my instincts to where I can act and react rather than overanalyze and shut down.

Having a mood disorder has helped me develop a sixth sense.

One of my bigger challenges is to feel comfortable when I'm alone or with people who aren't sympathetic. These are the times when I can spiral into negativity. Recognizing triggers, exercising fundamentals, and seeing the world with objectivity and optimism makes me more self-reliant and less dependent on others for validation.

The Essence of My Daily To-Do List

One of the main reasons I wrote this book is to give newcomers a crash course in how to better manage a mood disorder.

Here are a few of my personal takeaways that I think could help:

1. Choose to be free in my comfort zone instead of

feeling rigid outside of it.

2. Expand my comfort zone organically instead of forcing myself to be comfortable outside of it. This takes time, but I'm on a good path.

3. Do not live in the past anymore. After years of therapy, I've learned which tools I need. I ask the right questions too, even though the answers may overwhelm me at first.

4. Take it in stride if I am ignored. Sometimes I would rather be treated poorly than ignored. I lash out because my subconscious feels threatened and that can be triggered by being overlooked.

5. Stop forcing people to empathize with me. I need to encourage them to be empathic and not reject them for needing time to understand.

6. Remember that medication is a work in progress. It's not black and white. There's no perfect cocktail. All meds are different. Meds don't mean we're crazy. We don't need or not need them. When we take meds willingly, we are accepting the idea that we can be better. Meds are not the be-all and end-all. They're a step in the right direction.

7. Accept my past and learn from it. I need to be in the right mindset to accept change and understand that we all deserve to make our lives better. We all have reason to doubt and dwell on our mistakes. We must move forward with our lives.

8. Remember that self-actualization sits at the top of Maslow's pyramid. I need to feel secure without having to seek external validation.

9. Laugh at myself. When I do something stupid, I ask myself, "Who is this fool?" I must do this to keep perspective. It's crucial. When I screw up, I want to be able to laugh at myself right away, not years later, but in the moment. I want to do this instead of feeling like a failure who messed up again and resort to damage control by looking for a new job (or gym, or girlfriend). Clearly, I need to keep working on this too.

10. Understand that no matter how many hours of therapy I put in, I will always run into issues at work. Some people will see me as impossible to work with because of one incident or one bad day. I must take full responsibility and apologize to whomever I offend. I must learn from the experience to be better the next time.

11. Learn from my mistakes. I can keep repeating them in my relationships and expect different results or accept the fact that triggers will always be there, and I'm able to manage them.

12. Keep perspective. My therapist calls it "improving my 5 to 9" (pursuing meaningful endeavors in my down time) so that my workday, my 9 to 5, is more manageable.

13. Accept my shortcomings, attend groups, facilitate them too, and continue to do what I'm doing to stay positive and open-minded.

That's my list. Maybe some of it applies to you too, but if not, I would like to hear what does work.

Why It Matters

Guilt is a big motivator. So is love. I'd be fooling myself and you too, if I said that I don't feel guilty sometimes for putting my mom and dad (and others) through all the shit they've had to deal with for so many years. It's human to feel bad for putting our family and loved ones through hard times, especially when they try to be supportive.

To an extent at least, it's not our fault, but we *are* to blame if we do not acknowledge and try to accept the hurt we cause, and then take proactive steps to improve our mental health to respond better the next time.

I want my parents to know that what they've put up with over the past 37 years and what I've put myself through is not in vain. I'm getting better, even when I stumble occasionally. I want them to know that without being tedious or overly sentimental. I've put them through a lot. I had little to no idea what I was doing and how it was affecting them, but I do now. It takes little empathy to realize that keeping your mother and father awake nights, not knowing if their son is stable enough not to inflict self-harm, is wrenching and exhausting and too much to put on anyone.

It's also not hard to figure out that paying $45K a year for a college education when your kid racks up a steady diet of Cs is not exactly a fantastic investment. That kicked off my futile freshman year and continued for the next few years. I managed to graduate from an Ivy League school no less, but not with flying colors – more like a dull gray.

I lived at home for nearly two years after college since I couldn't live on my own. Once I made my way into the working world, I got fired multiple times, not for lack of technical ability, but because I couldn't handle the nuances of social interaction under pressure or the moment-to-moment crises that occur in most any business setting.

To protect my ego, I blamed everyone else instead of taking responsibility. I fought with myself, with my meds, with my doctors, and with my ideas. I was a hot mess until I tried behavioral therapy. Before then, I used my parents as a daily punching bag to diffuse my shit so I wouldn't risk going off on people at work – as if that's okay.

Perhaps I can never apologize enough, to all those I have hurt, at home, in school, at work, and wherever else I've lost control or gone rogue or weird or whatever you call it. I've done this in kitchens, bedrooms, classrooms, sub-ways, cafeterias, and parking lots too – basically, wherever I am and other humans gather. I'm not picky.

I was banned from a gym for throwing a towel at a woman who was talking too much to her boyfriend during spin class. During a meeting in college, I cussed out a club co-president because I didn't like his suggestions.

My moods have been known to kick in and dominate any place, any time, no direct reason necessary, and that can be scary for most people on the receiving end. This is not an excuse, just an explanation. I could go on and on, citing bad behavior and popping off endless apologies; but the point is, I have picked up many tools over the past 18 years, will continue to acquire new ones, and am obligated to put them to good use.

So Why Am I Telling You All This?

If I want to bring about any real change to the mental health landscape where I now live in New York City or anywhere else in the United States where help is desperately needed, I will have to stick my neck out, take risks, and be willing every now and then to come forward as a face of the movement, even when celebrity after celebrity (Catherine Zeta-Jones comes to mind) have been open about their own experience. As much as she and others are helping and appreciated, they are not in the trenches (to the best of my knowledge) like me and other facilitators and peer support specialists. So it's up to us to communicate directly with those in need of help.

Perhaps I'm writing this book as a means of rationalizing my history of behavior for the benefit of my friends and family. They deserve to know more than what I've struggled to convey in late-night confessions, early-morning emergencies, and incoherent emails and texts.

Unlike my school chums, I am not a senior manager in a high paying company. I feel content when I've done a good job in my 9 to 5; but nothing compares with the satisfaction from helping someone who struggles.

But my work has not been for nothing. From my work experience, I plan to leverage best practices from policy and procedure management and technology to organize a series of successful support groups. I plan to perfect my one group and scale it to several new ones while constantly re-evaluating and exploring improvement opportunities.

I'm convinced that other support group members can learn from my experiences, my mistakes (so many to choose from), successes (a few of those), and my general journey as a troubled kid, aggravated adolescent, and lost young adult.

Members of support groups, such as *Under 30* and *Friends and Family,* tend to rehash similar topics in each session without any follow-through. I would like to shorten their learning curve so that they do not have to suffer as much as I have. Listening to others' first-hand experiences provides that opportunity.

I've heard, "Why would you do this?" or "You should do that," or "Yeah, but listen," once too often from people who are trying to help but do not understand what it's like to have a mood disorder. These words are triggering even though they come with good intentions.

I think of a friend who committed suicide in 2015 and the many others who have or constantly experience suicidal ideation. She had been excommunicated from an ultra-Orthodox religious sect for denouncing her deeply religious background. She didn't have steady support for her borderline personality and bipolar disorder. Finally, she broke.

Incidents like this motivate me.

Like other volunteers, I have always felt inclined to answer the phone or respond to an email as soon as someone reaches out for help. Although I would like to speak by phone, it's impractical to talk to everyone all the time. I have done this on multiple occasions even when I have hours of work to do for early-morning meetings.

I want to create a global support system so that when I cannot draw members into my group, they can still feel connected, seen, and heard.

This means advocating for peer support and letting people know it is always available to them somewhere, somehow, in a formal setting or through one-on-one mentoring.

Why the Need for Support Groups?

I was fortunate that a group was there for me at my worst to help me through my share of extremely lonely scenes.

I was once removed from JetBlue's departure gate at the airport by 20 overly enthusiastic cops. The front desk associate made a mistake and couldn't board me on a flight to meet my brother in Vegas during the opening weekend of March Madness. We were just starting to rebuild our relationship and had planned to bond over the biggest weekend in sports – and on St. Patrick's Day!

It wasn't so much that the airline guy made a mistake; it was that he wouldn't own up to it. The combination of his indifference and perfect haircut triggered me, too.

(Oh the joys of bipolar.)

After screaming obscenities and absurdities for what seemed like several hours but was only a few minutes, I found myself exchanging verbal jabs and uppercuts with a cop the size of The Rock. He gave me an ultimatum: Leave now or he'd take me around the corner away from anyone who could observe us in another jurisdiction in a back alley where he assured me he would beat the mother-f-ing shit out of me.

Before I could contemplate his generous offer, another cop not quite as large but large enough, lifted me up and carried me to the nearest cab and told me to get in.

"Thank you," I said, meekly. I meant it. I know what a service he had done for me.

As I rode away in the cab, I realized I would never make it to Vegas to see my brother and we would have to explain Michael's latest debacle to our parents.

Rather than explore one of my self-destructive outlets, I chose group.

Even though I showed up late, the group came to my rescue when they saw me in a mixed state, manic and depressed, raging, and in tears. By the end of the group I stabilized, slept a much-needed seven hours, and landed a great job interview two days later.

When I Grow Old, What Will I Be?

When I look back on my accomplishments and failures, I don't want to miss opportunities to pursue what's needed now based on how much value peer support adds to people's lives. I've seen this first-hand in the many groups I have participated in, facilitated, and organized.

I will keep writing until that time too, because it's therapeutic, even when it's clumsy and lacks color, with crappy details from real life – because that's the way I've experienced it.

In the moment, it's messy and crude. Later, after editing and restructuring, it becomes coherent and enlightening. This may not just help me, it might help other people looking for help – the kind that only peer support can offer.

Bipolar is *Not* a Superpower

While Kanye West, with all his eccentricities, has made some interesting and valuable contributions when it comes to calling attention to mental health, especially mood disorders, some of his declarations are dangerously off-base and may do more harm than good.

Imagine a teenager at home struggling with bipolar issues, who is a big fan of Kanye, and he or she is watching a YouTube video of him going on and on about how cool it is to have a mood disorder and maybe how exhilarating it can be without meds. Then when the kid is basically all duped and ready to do whatever Kanye recommends, he goes on a rant about how bipolar is a superpower and that anyone diagnosed with it should just embrace it and keep off the meds and feel its full power and energy and just "go with the flow."

I respect Kanye's artistry, but not his character when he acts irresponsibly like this. Introspection, acceptance, and a lifelong journey to improve is what it's all about – not cheap thrills on the weekend, unwittingly encouraging vulnerable young people to do something reckless because that's just what being bipolar is all about.

A mood disorder enables us to be more empathic and supportive, which *can* be perceived as a superpower, especially if used altruistically, but it's not an organic, internal psychotropic drug to be used when it's time to sell a new album.

In fact, let's remember that there is no *happily ever after*, but each of us can be the star of our own movie and write our own script.

There really is no need to chase normal anymore. It's arrived. And it lives within each of us.

Acknowledgments

It feels as if I have been writing this book for my entire adult life, beginning with scraping together notes on Word documents, Evernote, saved emails, notepads, and manic texts written on crowded subways. Creating this book has been so rewarding but also has triggered painful memories. Overall though, the rewards from making amends far outweigh the hardships.

Working on this book has helped me to accept my past, forgive the people I need to forgive, and to remove the giant chip on my shoulder so I can move forward.

First, I'd like to gratefully acknowledge the time and effort from my Developmental Editor David T., and other reviewers and contributors.

To the Mood Disorders Support Group (MDSG) and its extended family where I got my start in New York's mental health community – thank you. Without these people, I would still be struggling.

Thanks to each of you:

Paul, chair at the time of MDSG, thank you for mentoring me and inviting me on the board.

David, one of my earliest wunderkind facilitators. I appreciate that you have a drier sense of humor than me.

Michael, for walking me through the best approach to create my own group.

Rebecca, for mentoring me to be a coordinator and showing me best practices to run multiple groups at one site.

Adina, you bravely put your mental health journey out there in your powerful one-woman performance. You inspired me to do the same.

Nathan, thank you for always calling and texting me out of the blue to make sure I'm doing okay.

Now, for those people who have *othered* me over the years: Without the adversity I wouldn't have the need to share my story.

As a media hound, I have several people to thank for their random contributions to my mental health:

Larry David, creator of the greatest comedic series of all time, *Seinfeld*, which perfectly captures my sense of humor – mostly my dry Jewish humor.

David Chase, for creating *The Sopranos*, the greatest series of all time. The dynamic between Tony and Dr. Melfi helped me enter into my first experience with psychodynamic therapy. They have also provided me a lifetime array of quotes and malapropisms.

Howard Stern, "The Media King" and greatest interviewer on the planet, you make every morning worth getting up for.

Melissa and Carla, two of the best behavioral therapists I know, thank you for pushing me to become a better patient and to hold myself accountable.

This brings me to my family:

Stuart, my father, you are the most tolerant and patient person in my life. Thank you for supporting me at every turn, encouraging me to be a scholar-athlete, and adding a little bit of Yiddish humor in our lives. Even more remarkable, I have witnessed you build a 50-year-long relationship with the strongest woman in the world.

Ivory, my mother, as the matriarch of our family, you have always been there for me. You attended groups. You accompanied me to therapy. You make me believe that I am the most important person in your world and showed me how devastated you would be if I ever lost myself. Your compassion and empathy allow me to persevere.

Jared, my older brother, and a guinea pig as the sibling of a bipolar person. We have not always been in sync, but I believe I am at my best when I feel closest with you. I look forward to the next shared chapter in our lives.

Delores, my loving aunt, you have the most supportive and loving heart of anyone I know. I gained a different perspective on life from all those weekends I spent with you in the *real* part of Philly. Thank you too, for sneaking me into R-rated films and indulging my lust for ice cream sundaes.

I'd like to address everyone who attends my group or any peer support group. I commend each one of you for acknowledging your truth by seeking new ways to improve your mental health. For those who do not yet have a nearby group, I hope this book helps you find your normal.

Lastly, thank you to everyone I played ball with who actually knew how to run a motion offense.

About the Author

For more than seven years, Michael J. Hoffman has been attending and facilitating mental health peer support groups in New York City, which address mental health and wellness issues in a secure, confidential, and non-judgmental forum. His background in operations, project management, and psychology has given him the tools to globalize a support group system similar to Alcoholics Anonymous and other 12-step programs. In his free time, Michael enjoys watching Philadelphia sports teams and making extravagant excuses whenever they lose.

Please contact Michael with questions
or to grab a cup of coffee at:
michael@peersupportny.com

For more information:
www.peersupportny.com